Building Levels in Unity

Create exciting 3D game worlds with Unity

Volodymyr Gerasimov

PUBLISHING

BIRMINGHAM - MUMBAI

Building Levels in Unity

First published: June 2015

Production reference: 1150615

Published by Packt Publishing Ltd.
Livery Place
35 Livery Street
Birmingham B3 2PB, UK.

ISBN 978-1-78528-284-3

www.packtpub.com

Credits

Author
Volodymyr Gerasimov

Reviewers
Dylan Agis
Attilio Carotenuto
Javier García-Lajara Herrero
Ryan Watkins

Commissioning Editor
Nadeem N. Bagban

Acquisition Editor
Meeta Rajani

Content Development Editor
Sumeet Sawant

Technical Editors
Vivek Arora
Deepti Tuscano

Copy Editors
Puja Lalwani
Merilyn Pereira
Laxmi Subramanian

Project Coordinator
Shweta H. Birwatkar

Proofreader
Safis Editing

Indexer
Tejal Soni

Production Coordinator
Manu Joseph

Cover Work
Manu Joseph

About the Author

Volodymyr Gerasimov is a game designer, developer, and producer who has worked on multiple titles in companies such as Holymountain Games, Best Way Soft, and Gameloft. Being introduced to Unity in its early versions, he continues to use and explore it to this day as a powerful, flexible, and affordable solution for personal projects and independence start-ups. His previously co-authored *Unity 3.x Scripting*, *Packt Publishing*. You can follow Volodymyr on his personal blog at `blog.vladgerasimov.com`.

About the Reviewers

Dylan Agis is a programmer and game designer currently working at Lifeguard Games. His current works include WellaPets and a few of his own projects. He has a strong background in C++ and C#, as well as Unity, and he loves problem solving. In the past, Dylan has also worked as a reviewer for *Mastering Unity 5.x Scripting, Packt Publishing*.

> I would like to thank Packt Publishing for giving me the opportunity to review again.

Attilio Carotenuto is an experienced game designer and developer based in London. After spending too much time playing games, he decided to start making them as well.

He's the owner and sole developer at Himeki Games, working on an unannounced hardcore game for PC, mobile, and console using Unity.

Attilio worked at Space Ape Games, making mobile games with Unity. Before that he was at King, developing *Farm Heroes Saga* and *EA Playfish* and creating social games and tools for the *The Sims* brand.

Attilio has previously worked for Packt Publishing on *Unity3D UI Essentials* and *Unity 3D Game Development by Example* as a technical reviewer.

Recent projects, tutorials, and articles from Attilio can be found on his personal website, www.attiliocarotenuto.com.

Javier García-Lajara Herrero was part of the booming video game industry in Spain, participating in the Commandos saga by Pyro Studios, where he developed as an artist and then continued his career in different disciplines at Virtual Toys, Bitoon, and Unusual Studios.

He is now one of the professors at U-Tad University of Technology.

Always passionate about technical advancements, he now researches and develops new proposals in games, virtual reality, and the aerial photogrammetry of objects and environments with drones.

You can check out Javier's blog at `blog.vladgerasimov.com` and follow him on twitter at `@Prf_Moriarty`.

Ryan Watkins is an aspiring light cyclist. You can find Ryan at `https://www.linkedin.com/in/ryanswatkins`.

www.PacktPub.com

Support files, eBooks, discount offers, and more

For support files and downloads related to your book, please visit www.PacktPub.com.

Did you know that Packt offers eBook versions of every book published, with PDF and ePub files available? You can upgrade to the eBook version at www.PacktPub.com and as a print book customer, you are entitled to a discount on the eBook copy. Get in touch with us at service@packtpub.com for more details.

At www.PacktPub.com, you can also read a collection of free technical articles, sign up for a range of free newsletters and receive exclusive discounts and offers on Packt books and eBooks.

https://www2.packtpub.com/books/subscription/packtlib

Do you need instant solutions to your IT questions? PacktLib is Packt's online digital book library. Here, you can search, access, and read Packt's entire library of books.

Why subscribe?

- Fully searchable across every book published by Packt
- Copy and paste, print, and bookmark content
- On demand and accessible via a web browser

Free access for Packt account holders

If you have an account with Packt at www.PacktPub.com, you can use this to access PacktLib today and view 9 entirely free books. Simply use your login credentials for immediate access.

Table of Contents

Preface

You've just installed Unity and don't know where to start, or simply wish to learn about new features that come with the fifth version of this engine. It doesn't matter if this is your first game engine or you are thinking of making a smooth transition to it, this book has got you covered. Throughout this book, you will be creating an outdoor environment, learning associated tools and features by following practical examples in a step-by-step fashion and solidifying your knowledge by completing practical tasks. Complementary files will allow you to start from any chapter you are interested in and also serve as a catch-up option if you don't wish to complete the tutorials. By the end of this book, you will know how to apply your knowledge of level design, animation, modeling, and much more to the best engines on the market.

What this book covers

Chapter 1, Meet Unity, introduces you to the Unity editor and basic tools used throughout the book. We will start from the very beginning by creating a starting project, discussing available windows, parameters, scene navigations, and package imports, and close this chapter with the challenge of recreating a custom window layout.

Chapter 2, Importing and Configuring Props, explains the process of exporting assets from 3D modeling apps and importing them into Unity, followed by their configuration, tuning, and troubleshooting common errors. By the end of the chapter, we will look into new materials introduced in Unity 5 and set up LODs for imported assets.

Chapter 3, Shaping Landscape, dives into the process of creating a terrain for the outdoor environment, as well as foliage, water, skyboxes, and trees.

Chapter 4, Dealing with Basic Animations, gives us the first look at how to handle animations in Unity 5. We will look into the Legacy system, the pros and cons of using it, import animations for the props, and use them to trigger scripts.

Chapter 5, Invite Your Characters to Unity, guides you through the entire process of how to import a humanoid character and get it prepared for the Mecanim animation system, as importing characters into Unity can cause a lot of problems if not done correctly.

Chapter 6, Using Mecanim for Advanced Animations, uses mocap animations and creates a basic locomotion state control to demonstrate the power of Mecanim.

Chapter 7, Lighting Up the World, explains what built-in Enlighten is capable of doing and talks about some limitations that come with it by lighting up an interior scene. Realtime Global Illumination boosted Unity's rendering capabilities through the roof. We will also look into other features such as light probing, reflection probes, lightmapping, projectors, light cookies, halos, and lenses.

Chapter 8, Bringing the Sound, discusses how the sound works and sets up the ambient sounds and music for our level using Audio Mixer.

Chapter 9, Exploring the Particle System, provides you with a practical example of creating a particle system, recommendations, tips and tricks, and a challenge to create your own particle system with provided resources. Although particles are fun, they can be overwhelmed by a variety of options available in the Particle editor.

Chapter 10, Final Editing and Build, enables us to get our character to walk around the level, talk about the project and quality settings, and finish with a playable build of our level.

What you need for this book

The only essential software for this book is obviously Unity 5.0.1. The example and tutorials shown are mostly incompatible with the earlier versions of Unity. A 2D drawing and a 3D modeling software will allow you to follow some of the tutorials, but are not essential. For the sake of accessibility, the examples feature both GIMP 2 and Blender 2.73, which can be downloaded for free; however, you are free to use any equivalent app of your choice (such as Photoshop, Maya, or 3Ds Max).

Who this book is for

This book is aimed at game artists who are interested in designing levels in Unity with no past programming experience and does not assume detailed knowledge of similar game platforms.

Conventions

In this book, you will find a number of text styles that distinguish between different kinds of information. Here are some examples of these styles and an explanation of their meaning.

Code words in text, database table names, folder names, filenames, file extensions, pathnames, dummy URLs, user input, and Twitter handles are shown as follows: "You will find more Detail assets to help with level creation within the `Chapter 3 | Details` folder."

New terms and **important words** are shown in bold. Words that you see on the screen, for example, in menus or dialog boxes, appear in the text like this: " Right now it is empty, so let's add one to it by clicking on the **New Project** button at the top right corner."

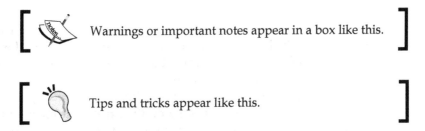

Warnings or important notes appear in a box like this.

Tips and tricks appear like this.

Reader feedback

Feedback from our readers is always welcome. Let us know what you think about this book—what you liked or disliked. Reader feedback is important for us as it helps us develop titles that you will really get the most out of.

To send us general feedback, simply e-mail `feedback@packtpub.com`, and mention the book's title in the subject of your message.

If there is a topic that you have expertise in and you are interested in either writing or contributing to a book, see our author guide at `www.packtpub.com/authors`.

Customer support

Now that you are the proud owner of a Packt book, we have a number of things to help you to get the most from your purchase.

Downloading the example code

You can download the example code files from your account at `http://www.packtpub.com` for all the Packt Publishing books you have purchased. If you purchased this book elsewhere, you can visit `http://www.packtpub.com/support` and register to have the files e-mailed directly to you.

Downloading the color images of this book

We also provide you with a PDF file that has color images of the screenshots/diagrams used in this book. The color images will help you better understand the changes in the output. You can download this file from `http://www.packtpub.com/sites/default/files/downloads/2843OT_ColorImages.pdf`.

Errata

Although we have taken every care to ensure the accuracy of our content, mistakes do happen. If you find a mistake in one of our books — maybe a mistake in the text or the code — we would be grateful if you could report this to us. By doing so, you can save other readers from frustration and help us improve subsequent versions of this book. If you find any errata, please report them by visiting `http://www.packtpub.com/submit-errata`, selecting your book, clicking on the **Errata Submission Form** link, and entering the details of your errata. Once your errata are verified, your submission will be accepted and the errata will be uploaded to our website or added to any list of existing errata under the Errata section of that title.

To view the previously submitted errata, go to `https://www.packtpub.com/books/content/support` and enter the name of the book in the search field. The required information will appear under the **Errata** section.

Piracy

Piracy of copyrighted material on the Internet is an ongoing problem across all media. At Packt, we take the protection of our copyright and licenses very seriously. If you come across any illegal copies of our works in any form on the Internet, please provide us with the location address or website name immediately so that we can pursue a remedy.

Please contact us at `copyright@packtpub.com` with a link to the suspected pirated material.

We appreciate your help in protecting our authors and our ability to bring you valuable content.

Questions

If you have a problem with any aspect of this book, you can contact us at
questions@packtpub.com, and we will do our best to address the problem.

1
Meet Unity

Welcome to *Building Levels in Unity!* This book will teach you how to build a complete level from start to finish in a step-by-step fashion. Designed for artists, modelers, animators, game designers, and people with no prior knowledge of game engines, you will find a lot of interesting information about editor functionality, asset import, character tuning, terrain creation, audio, lighting, and much more. Each chapter will focus on a set of topics, to build a solid foundation, and prepare you for more advanced material. By following the examples and using complementary download content, you will have a completely playable and tuned 3D environment.

In this chapter, we will learn the following:

- Learn to freely navigate in the Unity editor
- Create our first project
- Learn about creation and use of built-in primitives
- Use and purpose of GameObjects and everything required to deal with them

We will cover all the basics that are necessary for future learning and set up our project that will grow into a fully fleshed level. Let's begin!

Starting a project

I would assume that you've already downloaded Unity and finished the registration process. If you did, then by launching the program, you will be welcomed by the **Projects** screen where all your future projects will be located. Right now it is empty, so let's add one to it by clicking on the **New Project** button at the top-right corner.

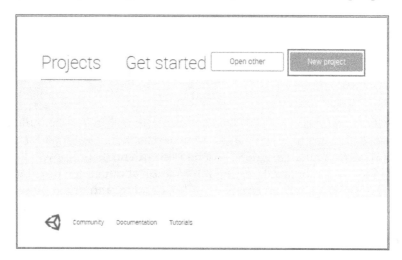

This will open a new window that will ask you to enter the name of your project and its location on the hard drive.

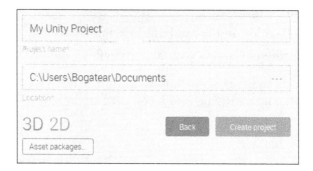

I'm going to skip the fancy naming and go with **My Unity Project** this time and leave the default **Location**. Make sure that you have the **3D** option selected, which will default our project to the 3D space and click on the **Create Project** button to proceed.

Don't worry about importing packages at this point; we can always do that later. If you already have a project, creating a new one is done by navigating to **File** | **New Project** in the top menu.

Windows

We are now going to take a quick look at the Unity editor and all its basic tools and features. You don't have to learn everything by heart at this point, especially if this is your first introduction to this engine; just taking mental notes about what's possible and what tools are available will suffice. We will look into, and study these tools in greater detail later in the book, so don't overwhelm yourself trying to remember everything.

Whenever you first open Unity, you will see a default layout like this:

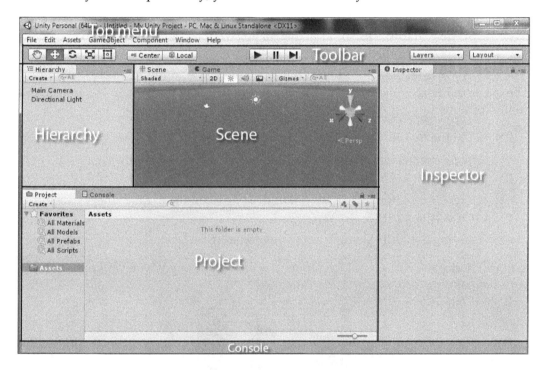

There are a lot of windows on display. We will be using naming conventions assigned to the windows in the preceding screenshot in all the examples throughout the book, so make sure to reference it whenever you feel lost.

The Scene window

The Scene window allows you to place, select, and edit objects in the level. It's like a sandbox designed for quick and comfortable manipulations of level building. This is where you, as an artist/designer, will spend most of your time working.

Scene navigation

There are a number of ways to navigate in the scene window, some of them you may find familiar from using other apps, and some are unique to the Unity editor.

Arrow navigation

Keyboard navigation arrows can be used to simulate walking through the environment. Move forward and backward with the up and down arrow keys, or pan left and right with the left and right arrow keys. Holding the *Shift* key will significantly increase movement speed. You probably won't use it too often, but it's a nice feature to have nonetheless. In order for hotkeys to have an effect, you need to have the **Scene** window selected as active, to do so simply left-click inside of it.

Mouse navigation

The most common method for navigation revolves around the mouse. Here are a few control options:

- Hold the middle mouse button and drag to pan.
- Hold *Alt* + the left mouse button and drag to orbit around the center of the screen.
- Hold *Alt* + right mouse button and drag or scroll the mouse wheel to zoom in and out.
- Holding the **Shift** key will allow you to navigate faster.

You will notice the **Hand Tool** icon in the **Toolbar** changing whenever you switch between panning, orbiting, and zooming.

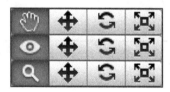

Flythrough

The Flythrough mode allows you to fly around your level from a first person perspective.

To enter the Flythrough mode, hold the right mouse button, and then use:

- The *WASD* keys to move forward, backward, and sideways
- The mouse to look around
- The *E* and *Q* buttons to go up and down

Holding the *Shift* key will allow you to fly faster. This navigation method is much more flexible then and similar to using arrow keys; however, it's still a lot more exotic than common.

Gizmo

Located in the upper-right corner of the Scene window, this allows you to quickly change camera orientation by clicking on one of the six cones, or switch between **Perspective mode** and **Isometric mode** by clicking on the text or cube in the middle.

Keep in mind that flythrough navigation is specifically designed for the Perspective mode. Gizmo is only available if you are working in the 3D mode.

The scene control bar allows you to choose various options for level viewing.

The drop-down menu (on the left) picks the draw mode for the scene.

The most notable three options of the Shading Mode are:

- **Shaded**: This is the default mode, which draws the object's surface with textures.
- **Wireframe**: This draws the object's wireframe.
- **Shaded Wireframe**: This combines both the previous modes with surfaces, textures and wireframes drawn.

Next are three switches that enable/disable 2D mode, lighting, and audio.

The effects button allows you to switch the following effects: skybox, fog, flares, animated materials. Clicking on a button will toggle them simultaneously; clicking on a drop-down menu will allow switching them individually.

The Gizmos menu allows you to control overlay graphics. You can toggle their visibility, control scale, and enable/disable the grid. This menu supports both built-in and custom gizmos created by programmers.

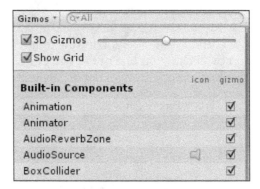

On the right is a search box allowing you to filter items by name or type. The searched objects will remain as is; however, all other objects will go gray scale and become semi-transparent, allowing filtered objects to stand out.

That's the basics of the Scene window. Most of these options are rarely used during development, but they do come in handy the closer you get to the polishing phase.

The Game window

The Game window shows the final representation of your level and how it will look in the game. Unlike the Scene window, you can set up custom cameras and show your game through them.

Play testing

In the middle of the toolbar, you will find three control buttons that will allow you to test your level in the game.

The buttons are **Play**, **Pause**, and **Step**. The first two are self-explanatory, the third one will play the game for a fraction of time before pausing and waiting for the next click.

Clicking on the **Play** button will activate the Game window, which will replace the Scene window.

You can switch between Scene and Game windows while testing, or placing them side by side to maximize efficiency, we will discover how to do that in future topics. That allows for a great amount of debugging flexibility; you can move objects, activate scripts, place enemies, all while the game is in progress. However, most changes made during the Play mode will be reset as soon as you stop testing, so be cautious when making those changes. There are useful plugins that you can download from the Unity Asset Store that will allow you to save changes made during the testing, whether to use them or not is completely up to personal preference.

Game window controls

The first drop-down menu controls the aspect ratio. You can use the available presets or create your own. This is especially useful if you are making a game for mobile devices.

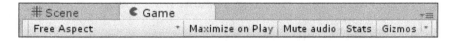

The following menus from the screenshot are explained as follows:

- **Maximize on Play**: This will toggle a fullscreen mode whenever you are play testing.
- **Mute audio**: This does exactly what you'd expect it to do.

- **Stats**: This will display rendering statistics, useful for reference when working on optimization.
- **Gizmos**: This menu is the same as the one in the Scene window. These options are very useful during play testing, they allow you to, for example, see triggers and raycasts.

The Hierarchy window

The **Hierarchy** window shows you the content of the level. All the objects that exist in the level will appear in the Hierarchy window.

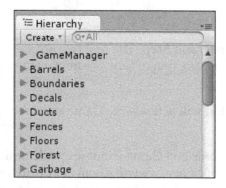

You can create new objects with a **Create** drop-down menu and quickly focus on them by:

1. Selecting objects in the **Hierarchy** window.
2. Moving the mouse cursor to the **Scene** window.
3. Pressing the *F* key.

This will allocate the camera and focus it on a selected object.

The Inspector window

Selecting objects in the Scene or Hierarchy window will allow you to add new Components, edit them and set up materials in the Inspector window. The Public script variables can also be edited without modifying the source code. All the operations regarding importing and some project-related settings will appear in the Inspector window as well.

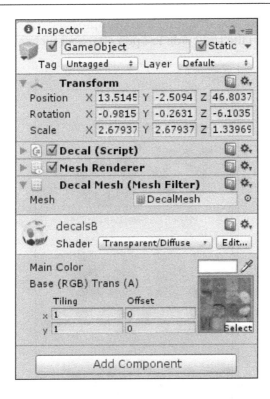

The **Inspector** window contains different types of properties such as values, references, arrays, colors, gradients, and curves. Let's take a good look at the first four of them.

Values are the most commonly used property. It can be anything: drop-down menu, checkbox, text field or even a slider. They are no different here in Unity then they are in any other application, just your standard numbers, Booleans, multi choices and strings.

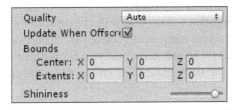

References, on the other hand, are slightly trickier. They require a reference of an object or a Component from the Project, Hierarchy, or Scene windows.

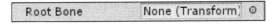

You can assign a reference by dragging and dropping the object into the reference field or using a circle on the right side to open an object picker.

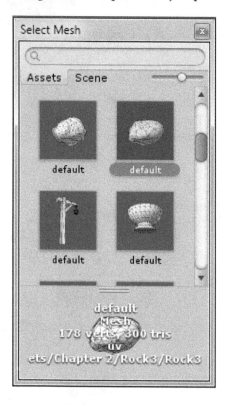

It's important to know that if the required reference type is a Component, you can sometimes reference an object that has that Component attached to it. The reference will be assigned to a first Component of that type. We will talk about the Components later in this chapter.

One thing you need to be aware of when dealing with arrays is how to control their **Size**. By incrementing the value, you will create more elements that will inherit properties from the last element of the array. However, decrementing the value will delete elements for good, so when you increment the size back, new elements will gain the value of the last element, not the value they used to have before decrementing.

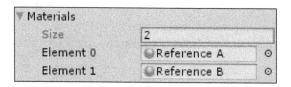

Based on the preceding screenshot, we can safely state that incrementing the **Size** parameter to 3 will create **Element 2** with assigned **Reference B** reference just like its predecessor **Element 1**. On the other hand, if we first decrement the **Size** to 1 and then increment it back to 2, **Element 1** reference will be changed from **Reference B** to **Reference A**.

Color is your usual RGB value. Clicking on the eyedropper tool will allow you to pick a color from the screen by hovering and left clicking.

Alternatively, you may select the color by opening the **Color Picker** tool and clicking on the color field. Here you can also create your own libraries of presets for future use.

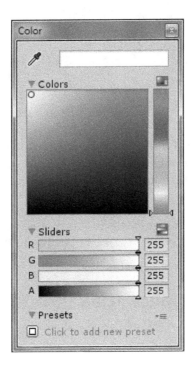

The latter two property types are not as common and we will look into them when they become relevant.

The Project window

This is similar to the Hierarchy window, however, it contains all the assets that exist within the project and can be used in the project.

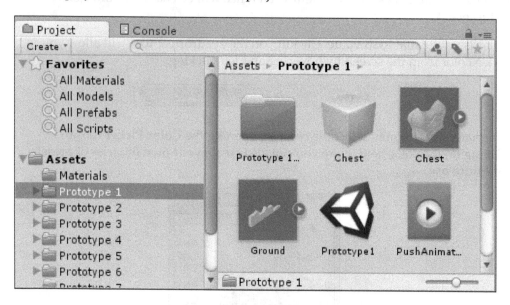

The default Project window layout is a new feature added with the 4th version of Unity. It's separated into two sections. The left side will show you a folder hierarchy and a list of **Favorites** (search inquiries). The right side will display previews of objects in the folder as well as the folder's location from the root, at the top.

From here you can select, organize, drag and drop assets into the Scene, Hierarchy, Inspector windows, or create new entities by clicking on the **Create** drop-down menu in the top-left corner.

Importing custom packages into the project

In order to continue working with this book's content, you need to learn how to import custom packages in Unity.

Packages are essentially a set of assets compressed into a single file. Packages help transfer data quickly and efficiently between different Unity projects or computers.

To import the package, do the following:

1. Right-click in the blank space of the **Project** window, alternatively, select **Assets** from the top menu.

2. Navigate to **Import Package | Custom Package**.

3. Navigate to the book files saved on your computer.

4. Select the **BuildingLevelsWithUnity.unitypackage** file and click on **Open.**

This will open the window in which you will be able to select files you want, or don't want, to import and then click on import to finalize the process.

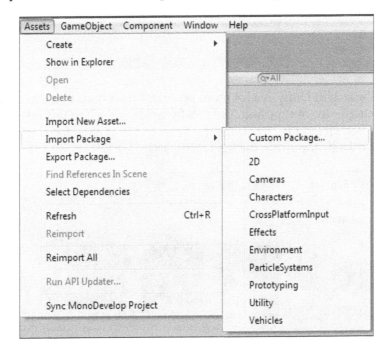

Now you know how to import packages to keep up with the book's material.

Search

You can sort the assets in the folders or use search to locate them by name, type, or labels:

1. Typing in the keywords in a search field will allow you to filter objects that have these keywords in them.

2. Click on a **Type** icon located on the right side of the search field to search by type.

3. Click on a **Label** icon to search by label.

4. Click on the **Save** button to save the search query to the **Favorites** list on the left.

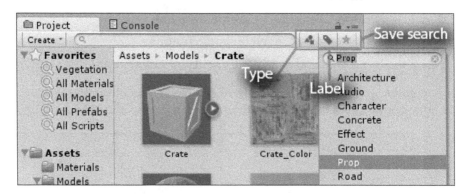

However, the search in Unity is a lot more powerful than that. You can combine multiple search queries of type and/or label by holding the *Ctrl* button or simply type them in a search field (t:typename for type, l:labelname for labels, searching by keyword works by inputting the keyword).

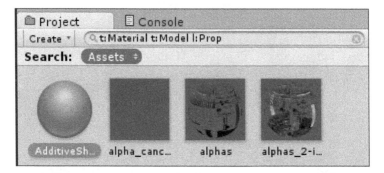

We will look more into Types and Labels in *Chapter 2, Importing and Configuring Props*.

Creating a custom search

Give this search functionality a try, and find objects that meet the following conditions:

1. Type: Texture and Model.

2. Label: Vegetation.

3. Keyword: Bush.

Give it a try and save the result as Bushes.

Rename

To rename an object in the Hierarchy or Project window, do the following:

1. Left-click on the entity.
2. Left-click again in the name area or press the *F2* key.

Do not double-click!

This is something you will have to get used to – double clicking will not enable renaming as you would expect, but may prompt to open the asset in the external application (for example, in the **Project** window, if you try to double-click on something like a texture file).

The Console window

The console will display a list of warnings, errors, and messages as they appear (mostly during play testing), that are useful to pay attention to because Unity can warn you about all sorts of things, not only code related.

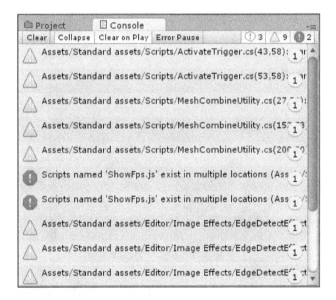

As you may notice, the Console window has multiple options available:

- **Clear**: This will clear all current logs
- **Collapse**: This will hide repeating logs
- **Clear On Play**: This will apply a **Clear** command every time you enter **Play** mode. It is recommended to always have it on.
- **Error Pause**: This will initiate Pause mode whenever the Error log appears

There is no need to have the Console window open all the time. The bottom of the screen has an area that will display the latest log in it whenever it appears. Double clicking on it will open the Console window.

Window controls

Windows aren't limited to just one instance. You can create as many copies as you like by clicking on a drop-down menu at the top-right corner of each window and selecting **Add Tab**.

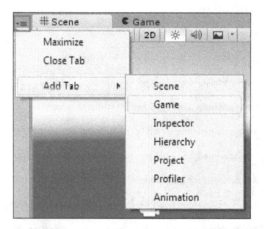

This is very useful, since windows like **Project** and **Inspector** have a **Lock** function (Lock sign next to Add Tab) allowing it to keep the current selection and enabling you to work with two objects at the same time.

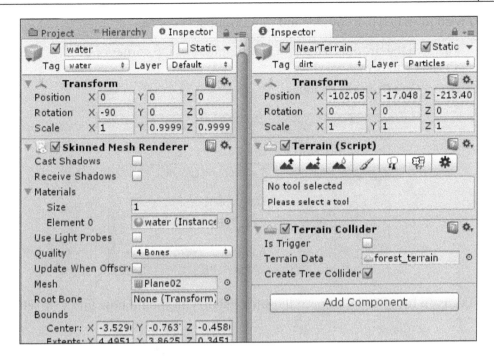

Changing the window layout

If you don't like the default window layout, you can change it anytime by dragging windows to different Docking Zones within the editor or drag them outside completely, to float.

There are a few layout presets that you may find useful. They are available under the **Layout** drop-down menu in the top-right corner of the editor or under **Window** | **Layouts** of the top menu.

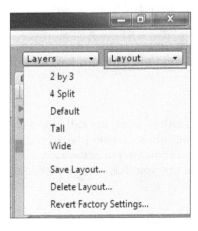

If you wish to switch to a simpler and more compact version:

1. Click on the drop-down menu in the rightmost top corner of the **Project** window.

2. Select **One Column Layout**.

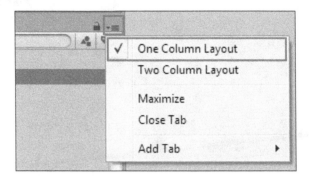

If you've been using Unity prior to the 4th version, you should now find yourself at home.

The only real downside of using **One Column Layout** is a lack of saved search inquiries.

From here on, we will be using the **Tall** preset layout with Project window set to **One column layout** (the drop-down menu at the top-right corner of the Project window) to optimize our screen space, but you can choose whichever one you like, this is a preference call.

Creating a custom layout

Just like with the search functionality, it would be a nice idea to solidify this knowledge with a practical example:

1. Revert to default layout by navigating to **Layout | Revert Factory Settings...** in the toolbar, or **Window | Layouts | Revert Factory Settings...** in the top menu.

2. Recreate the layout presented on the following screenshot:

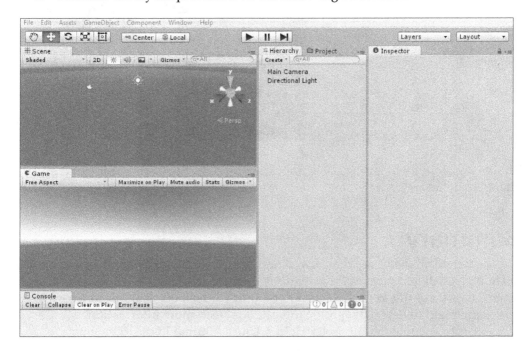

In order for this to work, you'll need to drag the windows around the editor in search of the invisible Docking Zones.

When you've customized the editor, save it by going to **Layout | Save Layout**.

The purpose of a Main Camera object

Cameras are unique GameObjects that serve as our eyes and ears in the game and the editor. By default there are two cameras—the Editor Camera and a Main Camera. The Editor Camera allows us to see objects in the Scene window and the Main Camera is the one we will be using during play testing. Sure, we can have as many cameras as we want and there are a lot of settings that we can play with, but at this point, it's enough to just be aware of it.

Creating primitives

Unity comes with its own set of basic primitives that can be created and edited for quick prototyping or greyblocking. There are **Cubes**, **Spheres**, **Capsules**, **Cylinders**, **Planes**, and **Quads**. They are available under **GameObject | 3D Object** in the top menu or under the **Create** menu of a Hierarchy window.

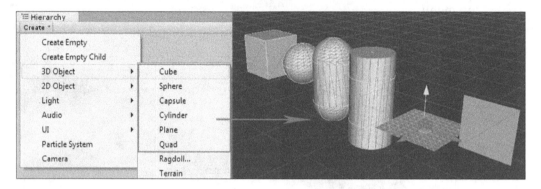

The created object will immediately appear, both in the Scene and inside of the Hierarchy window.

Summary

We've covered all the basics that newcomers need to know in order to be comfortable in Unity. Not all, but most of these features, tools, and functions will be used in the future chapters of this book. Whenever you find yourself lost feel free to return to this chapter and review that specific topic. If you need more information, use the official Unity documentation under **Help | Unity Manual** in the top menu.

In the next chapter, we will start importing assets and configuring them to be used in our level. We will discuss how to export your assets from other apps and how to configure them in Unity, and also set up materials and LODs.

2
Importing and Configuring Props

Before we start creating new, wonderful and exciting worlds, we need to import all our assets and get them ready to go. This chapter assumes that you have a basic understanding of modeling and texturing, and that you are also familiar with common terms such as UVs, normal maps, alpha channel, and so on. It doesn't matter which apps you are using for asset creation as long as they support exporting common file types. That is why you won't find any step-by-step export processes described for every single program, but only general recommendations and which things to avoid that are found applicable, regardless of you app choice.

In this chapter, we will look into the following topics:

- Object manipulation
- Working with components
- Importing props into Unity
- Configuring meshes
- Configuring textures
- Learning how to use Unity materials
- Setting up LODs for various objects
- Basics of collision

By the end of this chapter, you should be able to import all your props and prepare them to be used in the level.

Object manipulation

Learning to use the following tools will allow you to place objects in a **Scene** window with ease.

To test out the object manipulation tools, make sure you create one of the available 3D primitives in Unity via **GameObject | 3D Object** (**Cube** is recommended).

Object manipulation is done via five tools available on the left side of the toolbar:

- **Hand tool** (used for panning), **Move tool**, **Rotation tool**, **Scale tool**, and **Rect tool** can be accessed via the toolbar or by using the hotkeys *Q, W, E, R, T* respectively

- To duplicate an object, you can use *Ctrl+D* or a combination of *Ctrl+C* and *Ctrl+V* to copy and paste

- You can undo the last action via the *Ctrl+Z* combination

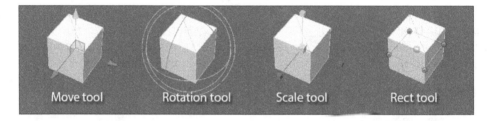

Rect tool is a recent addition that made an appearance in the later versions of Unity 4. The circle in the center of the object acts as the **Move tool** and a quad created with four dots on the outside works similar to the **Scale tool**. Dot location will change position based on the camera angle.

In addition, the toolbar contains tools that allow changing the pivot point of the object to its center or default pivot (useful if you imported the object with specific pivot point placement in mind). Objects can also be rotated, scaled, or moved relative to the **Local** or **Global** space. Settings are defaulted to **Pivot** translation in **Global** space

Snapping

Moving, rotating or scaling objects at equal intervals can be done via snapping. This is done by holding the *Ctrl* button.

To set the snapping intervals, go to **Edit | Snap settings** of the top menu and enter the following settings:

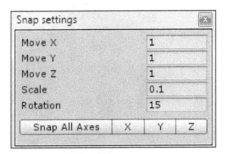

The buttons at the bottom of the **Snap settings** window allow you to round up to get rid of decimal values; it's great for if you wish objects to be perfectly aligned on the grid.

To move objects freely, press and hold *Shift* and use the **Move tool**. To move along the surface with a custom pivot point:

1. Select an object.
2. Hold *V.*
3. Position the pivot point with a mouse.
4. Hold and drag the left mouse button along the surface.

This is perfect for prop placement. As shown in the following screenshot:

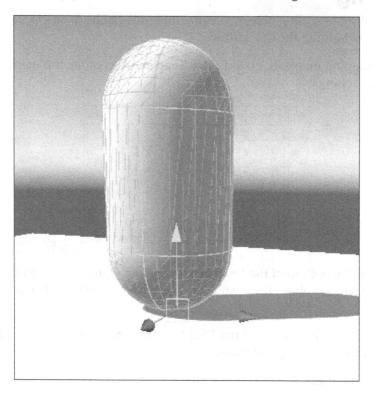

Surface snapping may sound like a lot of fun, but in reality, its results may vary based on surface and object topology; it's also very tricky to do in **Perspective** mode.

 Remember: Snapping works only in the Scene window.

Greyblocking

Knowing this much about Unity, we can utilize our knowledge of creating primitives by constructing a greyblock of our future level. Using Unity primitives, block out the level to solidify your knowledge of object manipulation.

Components

All objects in the level are GameObjects: entities that don't do much by themselves but serve as containers for parameters. These parameters are added with the help of components. If you create an empty GameObject via **GameObject | Create Empty** and look at the **Inspector** window, you will find that it contains one mandatory component called **Transform**, which houses properties mandatory for a 3D space (**Position, Rotation, Scale**). But that is all there is to it; GameObject is just an abstract entity that occupies a location in the Scene. In order to transform it to something more meaningful, more properties, and therefore, more components need to be added.

Adding components

By adding more components, we will add more properties to our GameObjects, so let's do just that and try to reconstruct a primitive:

1. Create an empty GameObject by going to **GameObject | Create Empty** in the top menu.
2. Click **Add Component** in the **Inspector** window or **Component | Add** in the top menu.
3. Go to **Mesh | Mesh Filter**.
4. Assign a **Cube** model reference to a **Mesh** property of a component through the object picker.
5. Add a new component via **Mesh | Mesh Renderer**.

At this point a purple cube should have appeared in place of your empty GameObject.

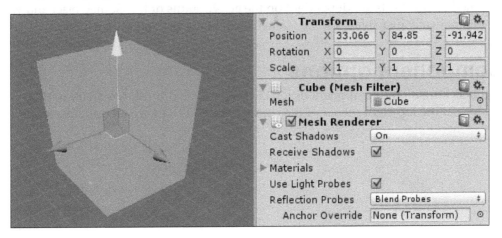

The **Mesh Filter** component allows us to set a mesh to represent the object in the level. **Mesh Renderer** adds rendering properties for this mesh, allowing it to be rendered in the **Scene** and **Game** window.

 If you see an object rendered purple, it's most likely because it doesn't have a material selected for it. We will look into **Materials** later in this chapter.

Component deactivation

One way to get rid of the GameObjects is by deleting them. However, that's very inefficient to do during runtime, and sometimes you'll find yourself needing to bring the removed object back. The best way to do that is by activating/deactivating the GameObject. To do that, toggle the check box next to the **Name** field at the top of the **Inspector** window. Some components can also be deactivated in a similar manner. That way, deactivation of the **Mesh Renderer** attached to our cube will cause it to disappear in the **Scene** window.

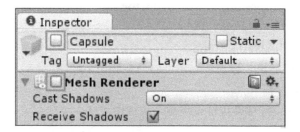

Attached components are dependent on the active status of the GameObject and will be automatically deactivated if the GameObject housing them is deactivated.

Component options

Right-clicking on the component or left clicking on the drop-down menu with a cog icon at the top-right corner of the component will bring up an options menu as seen here:

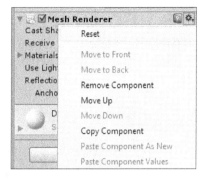

The most notable options are:

- **Reset**: This returns parameters to their default values
- **Remove Component**: This removes components from the GameObject
- **Copy Component**: This copies the component and its values
- **Paste Component As New**: This adds the copied component with copied values
- **Paste Component Values**: This transfers copied values to another component (only if the component is of the same type)

Objects that share the same components can be edited simultaneously. Selecting multiple objects will result in the **Inspector** window showing only shared components. Parameters will be left as they are if their values are the same for all selected objects, or they will be substituted with a dash if they don't match. Modifying a parameter will change it for all of the objects, as shown in the following screenshot:

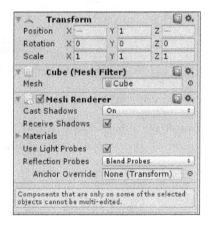

There are various components available, and we will look into most of them in future chapters.

Importing props into Unity

Unity handles the importing of assets quite smoothly, and there aren't that many issues that you will encounter, as long as the actual assets are without issues themselves.

Supported formats

Firstly, we will talk about 3D formats that are recognized by Unity.

Unity supports a number of common 3D file formats, namely: .FBX, .dae, .dxf, and .obj.

Among 3D application files, Unity supports 3Ds Max, Maya, Blender, Cinema4D, Modo, Lightwave, Cheetah3D, and many more (through conversion). Chances are that your preferred modeling tool is among them.

 Deciding which application to use is completely up to you, as there are a number of pros and cons when dealing with each.

When exporting into common 3D file formats (.obj for example), you will gain the advantage of:

- Having smaller file sizes.
- Being able to export from 3D apps that aren't supported by Unity.
- Being able to handpick the data you want to export.

However, there are few cons to that approach:

- They are harder to iterate.
- It is easy to lose track of versions between source and game data.

When using file formats native to your 3D app, you will benefit from the following:

- You will be able to iterate on the assets quickly (editing the imported asset will cause Unity to reimport it upon committing changes and returning it to the Editor).
- It's simple (there are no prerequisites to it, just drag and drop the file you were working on and open it from Unity for quick modification).

But there are few things that you will have to keep in mind:

- A licensed copy of a 3D app is required to open them.
- Along with assets, you may import unnecessary data.
- Files are generally bigger and may slow down Unity.
- Less validation will make it harder to troubleshoot errors.

 Exporting in a 3D app file format is justified during the prototyping, when you are constantly iterating, and all members of your team have a licensed version of the app installed.

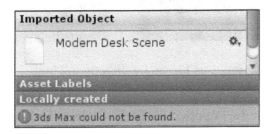

Exporting from Blender

As mentioned before, Unity supports import from popular 3D apps, and Blender is no exception. There is one thing that you need to be wary of when importing a Blender file into Unity; your Blender version has to be 2.45 or higher. The reason for this is that Unity uses the Blender FBX exporter added to Blender in version 2.45. If you are using an older version of Blender, you need to manually convert your files to a common 3D file format before importing.

 This is not just the case with Blender. If your 3D app doesn't have a built-in exporter, Unity will not be able to read the native file format. That is also the reason why you need to have that 3D software installed on a computer in order to access imported assets.

Object setup before exporting

In terms of the mesh, there aren't any Unity specific requirements that need to be met to import successfully.

If the asset that you are importing has multiple components and/or groups, make sure to set them up properly in a 3D app, as it will have the same hierarchy when imported into Unity.

You cannot modify an asset or its hierarchy directly in Unity. Say you've imported a .blend file into Unity and wish to edit it:

1. Double-click on the imported file in the **Project** window.
2. If you have Blender installed on your computer, Unity will opt to run it.
3. Edit the file and save it.
4. Return to the editor.

Once you've returned to the Editor, you might experience a small lag; that's Unity reimporting the file you've just edited.

Make sure that there is a pivot point where you want it to be. Remember, in Unity, the default is a center pivot point, but you can switch it to the one set in the 3D app, by going into Pivot mode.

Make sure that you remove construction history — Nurbs, Norms, and Subdiv surfaces must be converted into polygons. During the final export, get rid of your scene lighting; it will not be exported.

There are a few tips and tricks that you can apply in order to optimize your models, however, we will touch upon them later, after covering all related material.

The importing process

The easiest way to get assets, is simply by dragging and dropping the file into the **Project** window. It will create a copy of the file within the Unity directory. Alternatively, you can go to **Assets | Import New Asset...** in the top menu and import it that way.

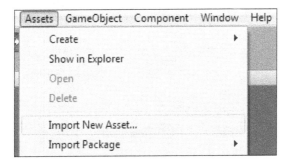

Files will be automatically converted, so you don't have to change anything else. Your asset is now in Unity and is ready to be used. To start things off, we need to do the following:

1. Open the **Chapter 2** folder of complimentary files.

2. Drag and drop the **Import** folder into the **Chapter 2** folder in the **Project** tab of Unity.

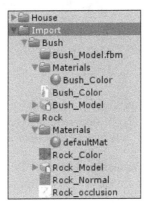

Congratulations! You've just imported OBJ and FBX models as well as PNG textures into Unity.

Configuring meshes

Now that we have our assets in, it's about time we started configuring them in Unity.

Model-meshes options

Selecting asset in **Project** window will display **Import settings** in the **Inspector** window.

Import settings have three tabs available corresponding to **Model**, **Rig**, and **Animation** settings of the asset. Right now, we will focus on the **Model** tab and look into available settings to prepare our asset to be used:

- **Scale factor**: This scales an asset in comparison to the original model. This is a great way to adjust a model's scale outside of a 3D modeling app. Using the **Scale Factor** parameter over **Scale tool** is also beneficial as it ensures that the object will correctly respond to physical interaction within Unity by using uniform scaling (developers report fixing this in Unity 5).

- **Mesh Compression**: Unity will attempt to reduce the size of the **Mesh. Compression** has four states: **Off**, **Low**, **Medium**, and **High**. To minimize your build size, try to use maximum compression until you see any irregularities appearing on the model.

In case you are wondering how compression works, the numerical accuracy of the mesh is reduced: instead of 32-bit floats, mesh data will be represented with a fixed number.

- **Read/Write Enabled**: This enables the meshes to be written at runtime. Enabling this option will allow mesh modifications through code. This is another optimization option that allows saving memory by turning it off for all meshes that aren't intended to be scaled or instantiated at runtime with a non-uniform scale.

- **Optimize Mesh**: This optimizes the order in which triangles will be listed in the mesh. Check it if you wish to trade loading time for a better runtime performance and vice versa.

- **Import BlendShapes**: Unity will import blend shapes for the model if this is enabled.

- **Generate Colliders**: This automatically generates a **Mesh Collider** for the model. It is useful for environment geometry. However, it should be avoided for any dynamic objects that will be moving.

- **Swap UVs**: This swaps primary and secondary UV channels.

- **Generate Lightmap UVs**: This creates a secondary UV channel for Lightmapping.

- **Normals & Tangents** are very straightforward options: you either **Import** info on **Normals & Tangents** from the source file, allow Unity to **Calculate** them for you (**Normals** are calculated based on the **Smoothing Angle** slider that sets how sharp the edge has to be in order to be treated as a Hard Edge) or choose **None** to disable them.

  Make sure to use the **Calculate** option on **Normals** if you need a quick fix for a model. Unity does a pretty good job of it.

 The import option on **Tangents** is available only for FBX, Maya, and 3Ds Max files.

- **Split Tangents**: Enable this if Normal Map lighting is broken by seams on your mesh.

- **Keep Quads**: This preserves quads on model topology for DirectX 11 tessellation.

Double-sided normals

There is one particular problem that you might run into when importing your models and try to view them in Unity. The problem lies in the fact that Unity, by default, doesn't support double-sided normals, making one side invisible. This is quite a regular problem, and there are a couple of ways to approach it. Have a programmer write a double-sided shader, use duplicate faces or reverse normals on your model in the 3D app. The latter is a lot easier, and a quicker way to solve this problem.

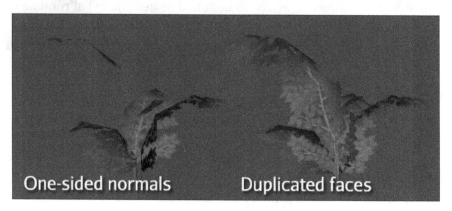

Labels

Now to the most important part of handling assets: **Labels**.

Labels are used for filtering and search queries. You can assign as many labels as you want to any asset, imported or internal. To do that:

1. Select the asset in the **Project** window.
2. Open the **Inspector** window.
3. Click on the **Label** button in the bottom-right corner of the **Preview** window.
4. Type in the label name.
5. Press *Enter* to create a new label and assign it to the object.

 Now you can use the search field of the project window to find the asset with the newly created label as shown in the following screenshot.

That's it. Labels are easy to understand. However, getting used to working with them and figuring out a system that you will use to filter through assets quickly will take some time.

Prefabs

Let's say you've configured a GameObject and its components, and you now want to reuse it multiple times throughout the project. Duplication is an option; however, there is a much better way, in the form of prefabs.

Think about prefabs as templates—they are generally used to create instances of certain objects and quickly modify them by applying changes made to the templates.

Creating prefabs is easy:

1. Click on the **Create** button of the **Project** window.
2. Select **Prefab**.
3. Drag and drop a primitive created earlier onto the prefab.

Done! Now you can observe how the prefab works. Notice that our original primitive in the Scene window now gained a new section called **Prefab** at the top of the **Inspector** window with three options available:

- **Select** will select a prefab that this object belongs to in the **Project** window.
- **Revert** will reset all changes done to the object and make it identical to the prefab.
- **Apply** will update the prefab with changes done to the object.

Try creating more instances of the prefab in the Scene, manipulate the prefab and use object transform, add and remove components from the prefab and objects, and see how they affect each other.

You should figure out that all objects are immediately updated whenever the prefab is changed, but a change done to a single object doesn't affect the prefab itself, unless changes are committed via the **Apply** button.

 If by any chance you forgot what you've changed in the object, there is no need to compare it to the prefab to find out; all changes will be highlighted in the Inspector window.

If you want to reset a particular component of an object from a prefab, you can do that by right-clicking on the component you wish to reset and select **Revert To Prefab**. This will reset that particular component only and leave other components untouched.

Objects that are connected to their prefabs will also be highlighted in the **Hierarchy** window with a blue color.

One thing to be cautious about is dragging and dropping an object onto a non-empty prefab, which will result in the replacement of all of its instances with the object you've dropped. This cannot be reverted with the *Ctrl+Z* command, but you will receive a warning message from Unity and can still cancel the action; so be wary.

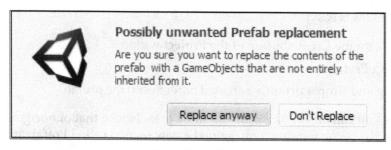

As a rule of thumb, it's a good precaution to set up all the objects to have their own prefabs, even if you aren't planning to mass modify them. There are two major reasons to do this:

1. Meshes cannot be modified, nor do they have components attached to them in the **Project** window. You can only do that by dragging the mesh into the Scene, which will automatically create a GameObject that you can then modify. Or, skip that and create a prefab editable in the **Project** window.

2. Programmers will have a much easier time working with cooked prefabs rather than manually assembling the required GameObject via code.

That being said, you should probably go ahead and create prefabs for the **Bush_Model** and **Rock_Model** assets we've recently imported. We'll need them very soon.

Object parenting

You can group objects by parenting them to other GameObjects, empty or not. In Unity, it can be done by dragging and dropping the GameObjects on top of each other in the Project or Hierarchy window.

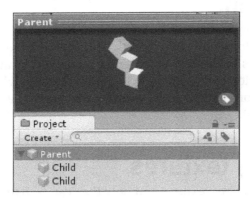

There is one thing to be aware of: it is important to understand that the transformation of the child is no longer relative to the global space, but to its parent object. So whenever the parent object moves, it will move all its children with it. This is also the case for scale and rotation.

Parenting and prefabs

When it comes to prefabs, parenting is quite simple: You freely modify and add any children to the parent object in the Hierarchy view and then hit **Apply** for them to be saved to the prefab. However, unparenting a child from a GameObject will cause the parent object to lose connection to the prefab.

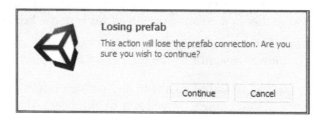

 If you need to use unparenting you will have to lose connection to the prefab for that object, unparent, and then drag and drop it back onto the prefab. That will commit changes to all other references as well.

The pivot point

Another important thing to know is how the pivot point of the parent object is going to react to the addition of child objects. This is where the **Pivot tool** that we've discussed earlier comes in handy. In the **Center mode**, it is located exactly in the middle of the group. However, switching to the **Pivot mode** will result in the pivot point snapping to the original position, where it was back when the parent object was exported (if it was).

Configuring textures

It's about time we talk about textures and how they can be handled in Unity. We will start by listing supported formats, discuss useful tips to consider during exporting, and take a close look at options available upon importing.

Supported formats

Unity has a wide range of supported formats for textures; they include PSD, TIFF, JPG, TGA, PNG, GIF, BMP, IFF, and PICT. Yes, multilayered files are supported, and you can easily use them without any fear of memory increase or performance loss. That being said, don't expect to be able to take advantage of a multilayered format, because Unity will convert the files and flatten all layers. This conversion is purely internal and your source files will not be altered in any way, allowing you to continue to iterate on them.

Preparing textures for export

There aren't any specific requirements for textures to be imported into Unity. If the image format is supported, drag and drop it into the **Project** window – just like we did earlier with the Import folder – and you are good to go.

From a performance standpoint, it is strongly recommended that you use the power of two sized textures (2, 4, 8, 16, 32, 64, 128, 256, 512...). The **non power of two textures** (**NPOT**) can be used in Unity at the cost of extra memory and a small performance loss. However, if a platform or a GPU doesn't support NPOT textures, Unity will automatically scale them to the nearest power of 2, causing a dramatic loss in performance.

 You can still use NPOT textures for something like UI.

Settings for various texture types

By selecting one of the imported textures, you will see import options in the **Inspector** window.

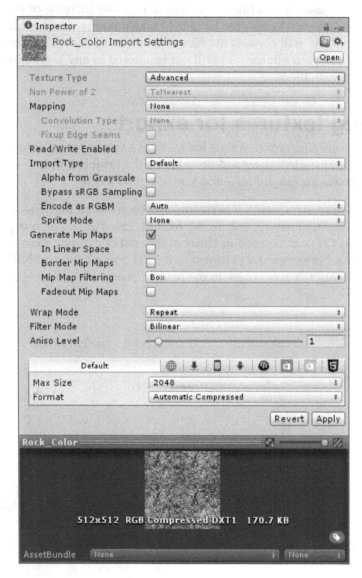

- Most of the settings of a texture are decided based on the value selected in the **Texture Type** drop-down menu. Here are the available options:

  ° **Texture**: This is the most common setting for textures (this is your default go-to option).

  ° **Normal Map**: This turns color channels into a format suitable for real-time normal mapping.

  ° **Editor GUI and Legacy GUI**: This is used for the GUI.

  ° **Sprite (2D and UI)**: Select this to use the texture as a sprite in a 2D game and UI.

  ° **Cursor**: This is useful for cursor sprites.

  ° **Cubemap**: This is used to create Cubemaps.

  ° **Cookie**: This is used for light cookies.

  ° **Lightmap**: This is used to identify lightmaps.

  ° **Advanced**: This reveals all parameters of the texture.

  Since the **Advanced** option gives us all the necessary parameters, we will stick to it from now on.

- **Non Power of 2** will define scaling behavior in case our texture has non-power-of-two size. Four options are available here:

  ° **None**: Texture won't be scaled

  ° **To nearest**: Texture will scale to the nearest power of 2 (`130x250` to `128x256`)

  ° **To larger**: Texture will scale to the next larger power of 2 (`130x200` to `256x256`)

  ° **To smaller**: Texture will scale to the next smaller power of 2 (`130x200` to `128x128`)

  All the changes will be applied upon import internally. After changing the parameter, Unity will re-import the texture.

- **Mapping** specifies layout options for custom Cubemaps and enables additional options associated with them. We will omit talking about Cubemaps as they are outside of the introductory scope.

- **Read/Write Enabled** allows coders to get access to texture data. Be careful with this one and keep it disabled by default unless it's absolutely required. This doubles texture memory usage due to the necessity of storing the edited and original version of the texture. It is only valid for uncompressed and DXT compressed textures.

- **Import Type** is a simplified version of a **Texture Type** parameter. It allows the texture's purpose to be interpreted properly and opens several options based on the type selected: **Default, Normal Map,** or **Lightmap.**

  ○ **Alpha from grayscale** is available for the **Default** texture type. It creates an alpha channel from the luminance information in the image.

  ○ **Create from grayscale** is available for the **Normal Map** texture type. It creates a Normal Map from luminance information in the image.

  ○ **Bypass RGB sampling** is for the **Default** texture type. It allows the use of direct color values from the image without gamma compensation applied by Unity.

  ○ **Encode as RGBM** does just that. It is useful for the HDR textures.

  ○ **Sprite Mode** allows you to configure your sprites as a **Single** image or a sprite sheet (**Multiple**).

- **Generate Mip Maps** allows the creation of smaller versions of the texture to be used when the texture appears small on the screen.

  ○ **In Linear Space** generates mip maps in linear color space.

  ○ **Border Mip Maps** prevents color from seeping out to the edge of the lower **Mip levels**.

- ° **Mip Map Filtering** is used to optimize mip map quality. The **Box** parameter makes mip levels gradually smoother, while **Kaiser** applies a sharpening algorithm to avoid blurry textures.

- ° **Fade Out Mip maps** makes mip maps fade to gray with mip level progression. The Fade Range scroller that appears after enabling this option defines the first level to start graying out and the last level when texture completely grays out.

- **Wrap Mode** defines the behavior of a tileable texture: you can choose to either, Repeat which will make texture repeat itself, or Clamp, to stretch edges (used by default for non-tileable textures).

- **Filter Mode** defines filtering options when the texture is stretched by transformation. **Point** will make the texture blocky, **Bilinear** will make it blurry, and **Trilinear** will blur the texture between different mip levels.

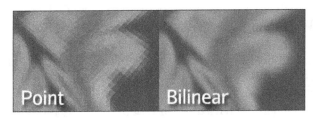

- The **Aniso Level** slider is available for Bilinear and Trilinear filters. It improves texture quality when viewed at a steep angle. It is most commonly used for a floor.

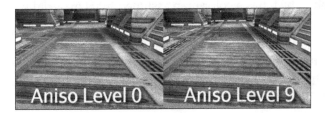

Getting your textures into Unity is as easy as it gets, plus you'll have a lot of options to tune them the way you like in the future. The best, and really the only, way to avoid being overwhelmed by the variety of options is to use **Texture Type** to filter them and base your decision on what's left.

Having textures imported is good and all, but it's not enough to use them with your GameObjects. For that we need **Shaders**, but more specifically their holders: **Materials**.

What are Materials?

Objects are rendered in Unity with the help of Shaders: chunks of complex code that can be created in Unity's MonoDevelop. However, there is a much easier way to work with Shaders, and that's through Materials. Materials allow the adjustment of properties and assignment of assets to Shaders without any programming knowledge.

Materials in Unity

Upon importing assets earlier, you probably noticed that Unity also created a folder called Materials in each asset folder. By default, each GameObject should have a Material assigned to it—if it doesn't it will be rendered pink, just like we've witnessed at the beginning of this chapter when tried to recreate primitives with components. During asset import, Unity used the name of the Shader assigned to the assets and gave it to the newly generated Material, which was automatically assigned to imported object; however, it didn't assign textures to both of the materials but only to the **Bush_Color**. There are three reasons why this could happen to any model:

1. Textures were not assigned to the Shader upon exporting. This is true in our case; **Rock** did not have textures assigned to it prior to exporting.

2. The file format was incorrect. That is also true. **Rock** was exported as OBJ and **Bush**, which has a color map assigned to its material was exported as FBX.

3. Unity couldn't find the assigned texture. That is not the case for our models, but it could often be the reason for others. To avoid that, I would recommend keeping models and assigned textures in the same folder upon import (you can always reallocate them afterwards).

Reassigning textures upon import can be a real pain. To avoid that issue, I usually:

1. Assign textures to the model in the 3D app.
2. Keep assigned textures in the same directory as the mesh file.
3. Export the model in FBX format.
4. Import the model and textures into Unity together.

This is not necessarily the only way to do it—you might not need to assign the textures in a 3D app in the first place for your pipeline, but this is just something I can recommend from personal experience.

In order to assign the missing textures to materials, we need to do the following:

1. Rename imported materials to **Rock_Material** and **Bush_Material** in the **Project** window.

2. Select **Rock_Material** and go to the **Inspector** window.

3. Click on the little circle on the left of the **Albedo** parameter.

4. Select the **Rock_Color** texture with the object picker.

Now all GameObjects that share this material will be automatically updated. You can use the **Preview** section at the bottom of the **Inspector** window to see how your material will look on the object:

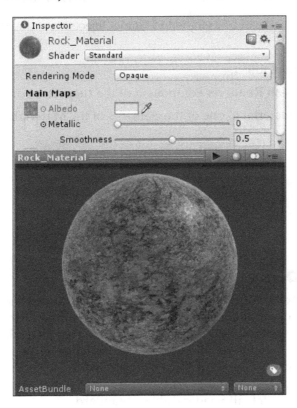

This color map will now be automatically assigned to all GameObjects that share this Material.

> You can't assign materials to imported models; however, you can do it for prefabs and objects in the Scene/Hierarchy window.

Creating Materials

Materials are very useful in a way that they are automatically updated on all assigned GameObjects. But at the same time, that is their biggest limitation, as we cannot create any variation this way. In our case, if we want to make some rocks darker and others greener, we'll have to create unique materials.

To create new materials, use the **Create** drop-down menu of the **Project** window.

Newly created material can be assigned to GameObjects with the **Mesh Renderer** component:

1. Select a **GameObject.**
2. Go to the **Mesh Renderer** component of the **Inspector** window.
3. Assign the material to one of the elements of the **Materials array.**

Shader types

The most important part of each material is to select the correct shader to render it. There is an abundance of shaders available for Unity, both built-in and user-created, available in the **Asset Store**. You can even write your own using ShaderLab coding language; however, that will require extensive knowledge of the subject. Thankfully, with the release of Unity 5, most of them were moved to the backlines for backward compatibility with project upgrades and were labeled Legacy. All of them were replaced with a single default Shader dubbed Standard.

Material parameters

Standard is a very powerful and versatile material with a lot of customization options that widen its application range.

Let's take a closer look at the options available for it:

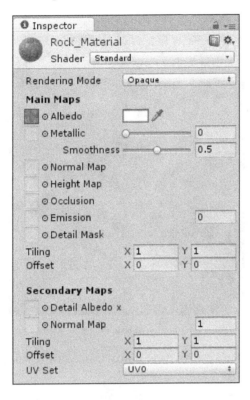

- **Main Maps** is a set of primary textures that are utilized by the Material:

- **Albedo** parameter defines a defuse color produced from the assigned color map and a surface color defined by the color picker on the right.

- **Metallic** defines how smooth and reflective the surface is. You can import a custom texture or use a slider to control how metallic you want your material to look. This parameter is further enhanced by the **Smoothness** slider.

- **Normal**, **Height**, **Occlusion**, and **Emission** are your standard maps for 3D objects. In this book, we will work with **Normal Map** and **Occlusion Map** for props and characters and we will use the **Height** map to generate terrain in the next chapter.

- **Detail Mask** uses the Alpha channel of the imported texture to create a mask for **Secondary Maps**. **Secondary Maps** allow us to create more details on the surface by importing in additional Color and Normal maps. Controlling the areas in which they will overlap is the purpose of the **Detail Mask**.

- **UV Set** allows you to toggle multiple UV sets if they are available for the model.

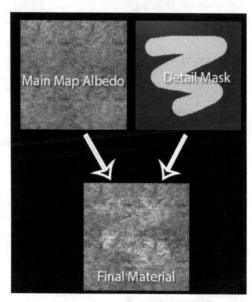

Here is a general idea of how the Detail Mask works

- **Tiling** allows us to control how many times our texture is going to be repeated across the x and y axes.

- **Offset** slides the texture across the x and y axes.

The last two parameters are best suited for tileable textures, like our imported **Rock_Color**. Increasing the x and y of the **Tiling** parameter to 5 will significantly improve the quality of our rock. Tiling has no effect on performance, nor does it require more memory to render the texture.

However, doing that will also create a problem when we try to apply non-tileable Occlusion and Normal maps to our model. To solve this dilemma, we will make use of both map-sets:

1. Remove the **Rock_Color** texture from the **Main Map Albedo** parameter and assign it to the **Detail Albedo** of the **Secondary Map.**

2. Set the surface color to a dark grey using the Color Picker next to the **Albedo** parameter.

3. Set the **Smoothness** parameter to 0.25.

4. Set the *x* and *y* **Tiling** of the **Secondary Map** to 5 (**Main Map Tiling** should be reverted to 1).

5. Assign the **Rock_Normal** texture to the **Normal Map** parameter of the **Main Map** and click the **Fix Now** button.

6. Assign the **Rock_Occlusion** texture to the **Occlusion** parameter.

With Normal and Occlusion Map assigned, our rock looks much better.

There is but one problem with this approach: secondary maps are much more expensive than main maps; therefore, Unity developers do not recommend utilizing Secondary Maps if Main Maps aren't being utilized.

While assigning the **Normal Map**, you've seen the **Fix Now** button pop up. This happens whenever you are trying to plug in textures to the **Normal Map** channel that weren't marked as such. Clicking on the **Fix Now button** automatically changes the **Texture Type** of Rock_Normal to the **Normal Map** in the **Import Settings**.

Rendering modes

As mentioned previously, the Standard material has four rendering modes that serve to fill the roles of different materials:

1. **Opaque**: This is used for solid or opaque objects. This is the Default go-to mode for most objects.

2. **Cutout**: This uses the Albedo alpha channel as a mask to isolate parts of the texture.

3. **Transparent**: This is used for objects with transparency, such as glass. The transparency parameter is transformed by the Albedo alpha channel.

4. **Fade**: This is very similar to the **Transparent** mode, with the only difference being that it also affects the specularity of the object, allowing it to gradually fade away by controlling the Albedo alpha channel.

To prepare our second model, we are going to rely on the Cutout Rendering mode of its material:

1. In the **Import** settings of the **Bush_Color** texture, check the **Alpha is Transparency** box. This will allow us to utilize the alpha channel to render leaves.

2. Change **Rendering** mode of the **Bush_Material** to **Cutout**.

3. The **Exposed Alpha Cutoff** slider will allow us to control the amount of cutout.

Using LODs in Unity

LOD stands for **Level of Details**. This is an extremely useful functionality that allows you to optimize your game by switching highly detailed objects with those of a simpler geometry, based on their screen space.

 LODs are toggled based on the percentage of game screen that is being occupied by the object, not just the camera distance, as is the case in many other programs.

In Unity, LOD is represented by an **LOD Group** component.

How to prepare LODs

In order to make LODs work, you need to have the actual models — more precisely, multiple versions of the same model that scale down in polycount. Here are a few useful tips to follow when creating LOD models:

- The number of versions is completely up to you as Unity will allow the creation of as many as you need.

- Keep object silhouettes relatively close so that players won't notice when models are being swapped.

Setting up LODs in Unity

To demonstrate how LODs work, we are going to utilize meshes that were imported with external package in the previous chapter. So make sure that you've successfully imported the package and have the **Chapter 2 | Ruin** folder in the **Project** window. To start up, let's do the following:

1. Create an empty GameObject via **GameObject | Create Empty** in the top menu.

2. Name it **LODParent** (not mandatory).

3. Attach the **LOD Group** component via **AddComponent | Rendering | LOD Group**.

As a rule of thumb, you don't attach the **LOD Group** component to the actual GameObjects you will be using as LODs; instead, you attach it to the empty GameObject.

Let's take a look at the properties that are available for the LOD Group component in the **Inspector** view.

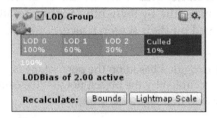

The LOD Groups at the top determine the number of LODs that this object has, and transition thresholds between them. As we've talked before, the switching is based on screen space and the percentages under the group names that represent the max point at which that particular LOD Group will be used.

You can create more LOD Groups by:

1. Right-clicking on the **LOD Group**.
2. Selecting **Insert before**.

Or, you can delete LOD Groups that you don't need by:

1. Right-clicking on the specific **LOD Group**.
2. Selecting **Delete**.

Thresholds are not fixed, and you can adjust them by dragging the LOD Group border and adjusting it to your preferences.

The camera icon above LOD Groups is a slider that allows you to manually adjust your camera to see the transition between LOD Groups.

Renderers is a list of models that become visible when **LOD Group** is active. To see them, select any LOD Group. You can add models there by clicking the **Add** button, or just drag and drop the model you want in there. To remove models, simply click the minus icon at the bottom-left corner. Another way to assign models to LOD Groups is to drop them into the LOD Groups directly. Every time you add new models, you will get a message from Unity about parenting the selected object to the object with the LOD Group. This is not mandatory; however, it's recommended that you do so.

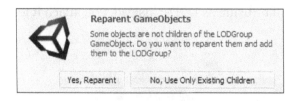

Bounds allow you to recalculate the bound volume of the object after the addition of a new LOD level.

Lightmap Scale updates **Scale** in the **Lightmap** property of the lightmap whenever LOD bounds are recalculated.

Drag and drop **Ruin** prefabs onto the respective **LOD Group** — all except for the **Culled** group. Culled is a point at which your model will be culled by the camera:

1. **Ruin_LOD1** to **LOD0**.
2. **Ruin_LOD2** to **LOD1**.
3. **Ruin_LOD3** to **LOD2**.

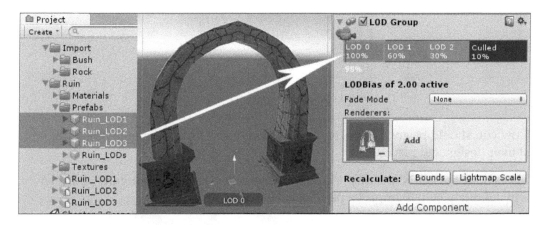

This will place the **Ruin** GameObjects in place of **LODParent** and indicate the **LOD** Group that is currently being rendered. You can now test the LODs with the camera slider and see models toggle as you pass the threshold.

LODBias

A lot of people are confused when they use camera slider because models don't seem to change at their thresholds, but at random spots. If that's the case with you, don't panic; that only means that it's working as intended and is being affected by **LODBias** parameter specified under **LOD** Groups. LODBias is used to adjust LOD Group thresholds to the quality settings of the game: the higher number will scale the amount of screen space required for LOD Group to change.

1. To adjust LODBias, go to **Edit** | **Project settings** | **Quality settings**.

2. Now, select your current quality level and change the **LODBias** parameter to 1.

Now you should be good to go, and your GameObject swapping models should be at their designated places.

That's it for the LODs in Unity. You don't have to use them in your game, but they will definitely help to improve performance when used properly.

Collider

Collider is a shell that is used to register physical interactions between objects; however, this will not prevent objects from moving into each other. Colliders are there to register collision, not to prevent it. To add a collider to an object, we need to add yet another component called **Box Collider** under **Physics | Box Collider**. The purpose of the collider is to register the collision between itself and objects controlled by physics and essentially to prevent your character from walking through walls and falling through the floor. Collider can be transformed manually by clicking **Edit Collider** button and dragging its boundaries

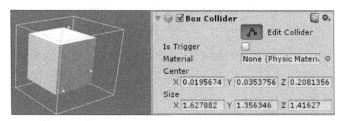

You might have noticed that there are a lot more colliders, but the **Box Collider** is the most commonly used one because of its simple geometry. Based on object topology and collision precision requirements, you might have to use multiple colliders by adding more collider components. The best results can be achieved by using **Mesh Collider**, which will copy the topology of the assigned mesh reference. But it is also the most performance heavy Collider and might cause issues if overused on dynamic objects.

Summary

At this point, you should feel capable of manipulating GameObjects, adding components, importing models and textures, and configuring materials in the Editor. Hope you've come to appreciate Unity even more after you've witnessed how simple this engine actually is. If you need more information on how to handle importing objects from any specific 3D app, you can always reference the official documentation available at `http://docs.unity3d.com/Manual/HOWTO-importObject.html`.

If you wish to learn more about materials and physical-based shading, I would direct you to the official tutorial at `www.youtube.com/watch?v=fD_ho_ofY6A`.

In the next chapter, we will look into Unity's built-in **Terrain** system and how to use it.

3
Shaping Landscape

It's about time we take that greyblock we built earlier, infuse it with imported assets, and build an environment around it, while also being introduced to the native Unity tools that will help us with the following:

- Terrain creation
- Terrain sculpting, painting, and texturing
- Terrain creation using heightmaps
- Using Unity water
- Learning Unity Tree editor
- Adding foliage
- Terrain settings
- Adding skyboxes

By the end of this chapter, you should be able to create your own exterior level and enhance it with forests, ponds, and foliage.

Creating terrain

It goes without saying that if you are planning to build a landscape, Unity terrain is the way to go. Being extremely easy to use and modify, this native asset is also optimized, allowing artists to push their creative boundaries even further than they usually can with imported terrains.

Our outdoor level will start with a base terrain that will replace a primitive we've used for the ground, on the greyblock, in our last chapter. To create one, go to **GameObject | 3D Object | Terrain**. This will spawn a terrain asset in your Hierarchy view and place it in the Scene.

Terrain is just like any other GameObject with two key components attached to it.

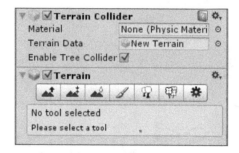

The **Terrain Collider** component creates a collider for the terrain. Though you can't see the usual bounding box around it, it's actually there. Its shape is defined by the **Terrain Data** parameter that has the terrain object itself assigned to it as a reference (**New Terrain**). This terrain object can be found in the Project window and is created along with the terrain. You can rename it or assign a different reference to the **Terrain Data** parameter; however, in truth, I can't see a situation where you would need to do that.

The **Enable Tree Collider** parameter is not that transparent; we will talk about trees in future topics and how to properly set them up. For now, it is enough to say that this parameter allows trees to utilize the colliders attached to them.

The **Terrain** component is a script that holds all the functionality and tools that you will be working with, on your terrain. This is something we need to talk about in depth, so here it goes.

Sculpting

The first three tools on the left of your toolbox are used for various sculpting purposes.

The tools are very simple and self-explanatory, as they allow most of their parameters to be altered in the **Settings** section, such as **Brush Size** and **Opacity**. These are percent-based parameters that are regulated with a slider.

Brush Size is based on the size of the texture it is represented by a parameter value of 100 and can be scaled down with a slider.

Opacity controls the strength of the applied effect and is ultimately based on a grayscale gradient of the brush texture; lowering the value will bring it closer to white. Whenever you are using these tools, what you are actually doing is painting the heightmap of the terrain which is constantly being updated.

Raise/Lower Terrain is your common go-to tool for terrain sculpting (the leftmost button).

- Holding the left mouse button and drawing over the terrain surface will lift it
- Holding the *Shift* key while doing that will apply the opposite effect

 You have to move the brush in order to keep reapplying this effect or simply click multiple times while readjusting the brush position.

The **Paint Height** tool will allow you to raise the terrain to a height determined by the **Height** parameter using the brush. It's perfect to create plateaus or if you are in need of greater control over the terrain height.

Holding *Shift* over a certain area will take a sample of its height and assign that value to the **Height** parameter. Clicking the **Flatten** button next to the **Height** parameter will bring the entire terrain to the specified height.

 One important thing to keep in mind is that you can't go to a height below 0 when editing terrain, which means that creating a hole in the ground will require raising the entire terrain first and then lowering the area of the hole with the **Raise/Lower Terrain** tool.

The **Smooth Height** tool averages the nearest height values to create a smoother looking terrain.

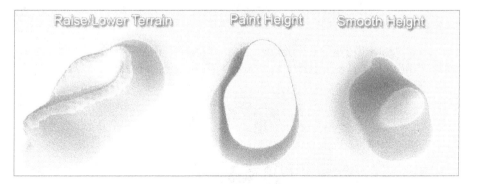

Brushes

All the tools that you are going to be using for terrain editing utilize the same set of default brushes. The number of brushes is limited, as such so are our options; however, we can also import our own custom brushes and use them.

Creating a brush

For this exercise we will use GIMP 2.8 to create a brush, but you can do it with any 2D app of your own preference.

First, we will create a new file; it doesn't have to be large—64 x 64 will fit just fine. If you can, you should specify that you'll be using grayscale colors and set a transparent background (Photoshop users can simply change to the grayscale mode and delete the background layer).

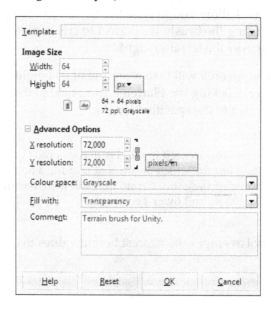

Using grayscale colors, draw whatever you feel like. Remember, the darker the value the stronger the effect of a brush in that area will be and vice versa.

Now, save the file in the .png format and call it brush_0 (naming is very important here). For GIMP users, go to **File | Export As** and select the **.png** format on export.

Importing a brush

Now, here comes the tricky part:

1. In the Project window of Unity, create a new folder called Gizmos.
2. Import the newly created brush into that folder.
3. Restart Unity.

Now you should be able to see your new brush imported into Unity and it should be selectable from the palette.

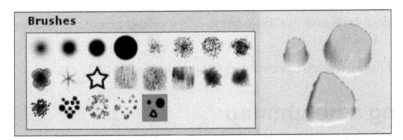

If the brush didn't import, here are some steps for troubleshooting:

1. Make sure that the brush folder is named Gizmos.
2. Make sure that the brush name is brush_0.
3. Make sure that the brush has .png extension.
4. Make sure that the Gizmos folder is not placed in any other folder.
5. Restart Unity.

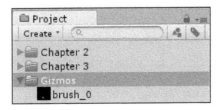

For new brushes, simply continue the numeration from 0 (brush_0, brush_1, brush_2, and so on). You can't start with anything but 0 and you can't change the naming convention; otherwise this will not work.

This is a perfect time to practice these tools because in our next topic, we will start editing the terrain for our level.

Creating the terrain using heightmaps

Scale is one of the most common issues that designers face when dealing with terrain for the first time. The process of fixing the scale can lead to a lot of frustration, and to re-edit large parts of the terrain, you can't simply shrink or extend selected areas with the default toolset; you have to manually redraw them. Thankfully, there is an easy way to get close to what we want in the first attempt, and that's by using heightmaps.

Heightmaps work in the same way as brushes; the engine interprets the grayscale colors as elevation data and applies it to the terrain. They can be easily created with any app that supports exporting in the .raw format (such as GIMP and Photoshop).

To increase our precision with the heightmap, we could take a top-down screenshot of the greyblock level and use the location of the placed primitives as reference points while drawing.

Let's look at how to create our own heightmaps using GIMP 2.

Drawing a heightmap

Start by creating a new image with the following characteristics:

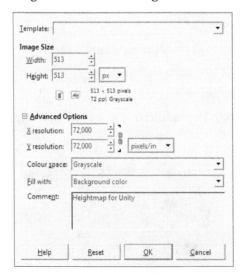

Heightmaps in Unity follow a very simple rule: their size has to be a power of 2 + 1 pixel (512 is your usual size, power of 2 + 1 will make it 513, which we are going to use).

In the case of heightmaps, we will be working with shades of gray, so going for a grayscale color mode is the obvious choice.

The actual heightmap is just a black and white image: the brighter the area the higher it will raise the terrain.

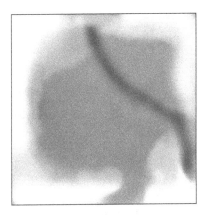

By importing the screenshot from the greyblock, we can easily tell where and how to paint our heightmap. Don't worry about how high the white areas are going to appear on the terrain—at this point, it's all about the tone and where you want the change of elevation to happen. In this example, we want to have a stream running across the level and allow the player to approach it by walking down the hill.

Exporting a heightmap

Now that our heightmap is drawn, we need to export it in the `.raw` format—the only format that Unity will accept. Follow these steps to export the heightmap:

1. Go to **File** | **Export As...**.
2. Under **Select File Type**, scroll down and select **Raw image data**.
3. Name your file.

4. Click on **Export**.

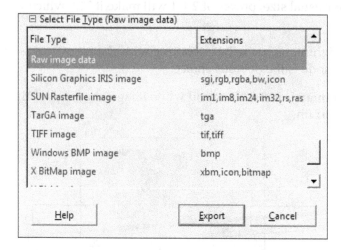

5. In the following window, make sure that you select **Planar (RRR,GGG,BBB)** option under **RGB Save Type**:

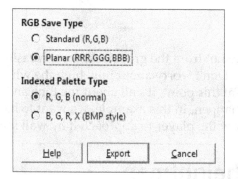

Applying heightmap to a terrain

Back to Unity! At the very bottom of **Terrain Settings** (rightmost tab with a cog sign), there is a **Heightmap** category with two options:

Export Raw... allows us to export the current heightmap and modify it.

Import Raw... allows us to use our own heightmap on the current terrain, which is what we are looking for.

Clicking on the **Import Raw…** button and choosing our heightmap will open an **Import Heightmap** window. For successful import, we need to make sure that the following options are set correctly:

- **Depth** should be at **8bit**
- **Width** and **Height** should correspond to the **X** and **Y** values of our heightmap (513 x 513)
- Depending on your operating system, **Byte Order** should be set to **Windows** or **Mac**
- **Terrain Size** can be left as is, or modified to your preference (100x30x100 in our case)

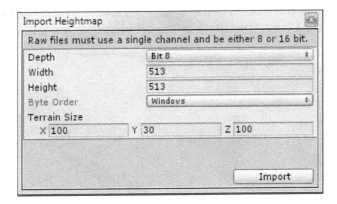

That should do it, and by the end of it, you should have your terrain shaped in accordance with your heightmap.

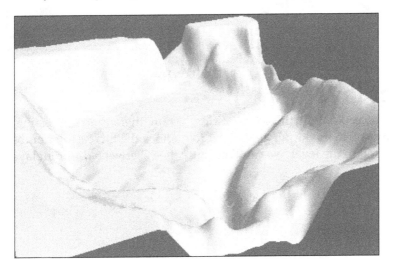

Drawn heightmaps can be a little rough, so make sure to invest some time in polishing it with terrain tools afterwards.

When it comes to heightmap creation, there are a lot of apps that you can use to generate them: Photoshop, Maya, Blender, World Machine, Terragen, ZBrush, and so on. GIMP 2 is used in this example for convenience since it's free and anybody can get a hold of it.

Level meshing

With our heightmap applied and terrain polished, we can start replacing the greyblock primitives with the actual objects that will be used in the final level. You will find most of the models in the `Chapter 2` folder. You can also download asset packs from the Unity Asset Store or import your own models.

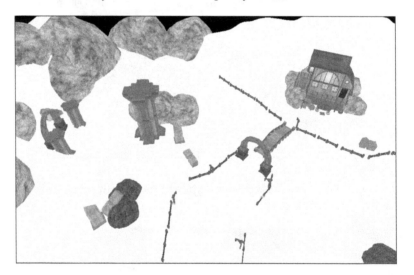

Object layers

Before we proceed any further with editing terrain, there is an interesting functionality worth mentioning. In order to manage the increasing number of assets added to the level, we can distribute them between different layers.

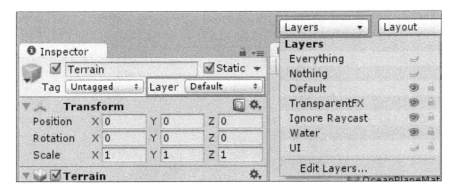

Every GameObject in the level is assigned to a certain layer, and you can easily change an object's layer by selecting it from the drop-down menu at the top of the **Inspector** window.

There are two major benefits in placing objects on separate layers:

- **Hide/Show Layer** allows you to hide/reveal objects in the editor. This is extremely useful during production as it helps you to hide the objects that serve a supporting role as visual indicators, like waypoints.

- **Locking Layer for Picking** is especially useful in our case to make sure we aren't accidentally selecting objects we aren't concerned with.

These options are available under the **Layers** drop-down menu of the toolbar. Now that we are going into terrain texturing, it would be useful to place all our assets onto a custom layer, lock it, and toggle visibility if needed.

To add a custom layer, click on the **Add Layer** option in the **Layer** drop-down menu of the **Inspector** window or; **Edit Layers…** under the **Layers** drop-down menu of the toolbar.

This will take you to the **Tags & Layers** window, where you can add new layers by filling in the **User Layer** fields.

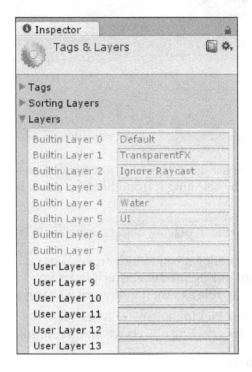

The terrain texture

Now that we have a terrain sculpted and models placed, it's time to add some textures with the Paint Texture tool.

Importing textures

For this example, we will use the textures available in the Chapter 3 | Terrain Textures folder in the Project window. In addition, you can also import some of Unity's built-in packages for greater texture variety.

1. Go to **Assets | Import Package | Environment**.
2. Click on **Import**.

This will import some textures for the terrain and tree models that we will use in the future.

Unity supports multilayered texturing for terrain. It's very intuitive and natural to grasp: imagine multiple textures being stacked on top of each other and all of them share an opacity parameter in a certain area, which allows you to manually increase the opacity of certain textures, and at the same time, lower the opacity of others. This is not exactly how it works under the hood; however, this is what you will experience when working with terrain textures in Unity.

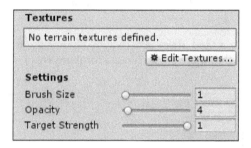

To add textures to the list, simply click on the **Edit Textures...** button and select **Add Texture**. This will open a new window where you can select a color and a normal map for that texture. Select **Dirt_Color** for the **Albedo** parameter, **Dirt_Normal** for the **Normal** parameter (terrain is currently using the standard shader), and click on **Add**.

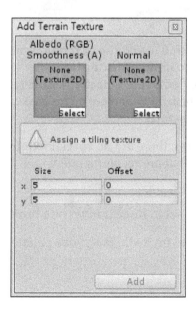

Options during texture picking are quite straightforward:

- **Size**: This allows you to scale texture up and down along the x and/or y axis.
- **Offset**: This just offsets it by a specified amount. You won't find yourself using this option that often, if ever.

As you can see, the terrain is now completely covered with this texture. Unity does this all the time; it automatically assumes that the first texture on the list is the default background texture that you want the entire terrain to be covered with, so keep that in mind whenever trying to decide on assignment order.

 Once added, there is no way to change the texture order (not that there is much need for it anyway).

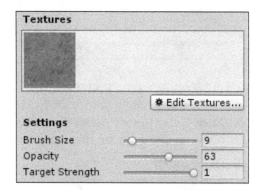

Texturing settings are very similar to those of terrain sculpting. One thing that you need to keep in mind is that painting a texture over the same spot will increase its opacity by the amount specified in the **Opacity** parameter (63 being 63 percent) up to a **Target Strength** value (1 being 100 percent). This makes it very similar to the Paint Height tool we've looked at before.

For your own custom textures, there are no special requirements that should be met. There are only a few things that are recommended:

- The texture must be tileable.
- Wrap mode must be set to **Repeat** in texture Import Settings.

That will do it. You can add extra textures to your palette and paint over the terrain while getting used to the tool.

Texturing the terrain

Try adding the rest of the textures from the Chapter 3 folder and using them in the level. How you use and combine them for your level is an artistic call. If you need a reference, you can always refer to the finished level inside the **Chapter 3 Finished** folder in the **Project** window.

Water in Unity

Unity 5 comes with three different water solutions; they are varied in the level of complexity and hardware requirements. Despite this variety, water in Unity is nothing but aesthetical. It doesn't react to physical objects or add post-processing to the camera when a character gets under it. But, I can't really count that as a negative since rarely do games require water to be more than just a good-looking plane. If you are in need of a more realistic solution for your project, you just may find what you are looking for in the Unity Asset Store.

If you have the Environment package imported, water prefabs can be found under the **Standard Assets** | **Environment** | **Water**, inside of which you can navigate to **Water** | **Water 4** | **Water (Basic)**.

We are going to keep the introduction to Unity Water short and focus on one of the available Water solutions. Find the **WaterProDaytime** prefab in **Standard Assets** | **Environment** | **Water** | **Water** | **Prefabs** and drag it into the scene.

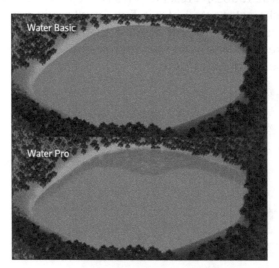

If we take a close look at the GameObject, we'll see that there are two things that are turning it into Unity Water: the **Water** component and **WaterProDaytime** material, that both contain important parameters to control Water behavior.

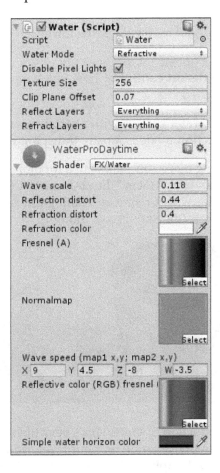

Water Mode has three options that depend completely on which shader version the user's video card supports:

- **Simple** works on most graphic cards
- **Reflective** requires pixel shader 1.4 support and above
- **Refractive** requires 2.0 pixel shader support

You don't have to worry about this too much as Unity will downscale the settings if any specific mode isn't supported. However, it does add additional work by having to adjust the settings of every mode, just in case.

Texture Size parameter and **Disable Pixel Lighting** are self-explanatory.

Reflect and **Refract Layers** allow you to pick and choose layers that you don't want to reflect on the water surface.

Wave scale controls the Normal map values: the lower the slider value, the higher the waves will be.

Refraction and **Reflection distort** control by how much the object reflected on the water surface, will be distorted.

Refraction color colors the water surface with a certain hue (helps to set the mood, because water in the **Refraction** mode is mostly transparent).

If you want to try something more complex with a lot more options to play with, try **Water4** under **Standard Assets | Environment | Water | Water4**. The **Water4Advanced** prefab has waves rising and falling as well as foaming around objects below the water plane (they aren't real though).

That will be it for the introduction of Water. It's a very niche and limited feature that works only for visual representation. For our level, we will continue using the **WaterProDaytime** prefab and duplicate it along the river bank.

Adding trees to the level

Populating our level with trees and creating forests can be done by using the Place Trees tool.

Let me get this out of the way right now: they don't have to be "trees" per se. However, it is highly recommended that you reserve your other foliage and environmental details that don't act like trees, for another tool that we will look into in the next topic.

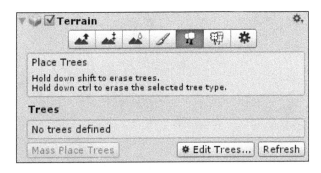

The customization options and uses of the Place Trees tool are very limited. Just like for other tools, we start with no objects in our palette and must add some to work with. For that, we go to **Edit Trees...** | **Add Tree**.

Now we can select a tree from the Object Picker from the new option window. Choose **Palm_Desktop** from the imported Standard Package.

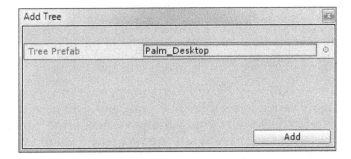

In here, the only option available to us is **Bend Factor**. This parameter will only appear/work if the selected tree was created with Unity Tree Creator – it adjusts tree responsiveness to the wind or how much the tree will bend if a Wind Zone exists in the scene (**GameObject** | **3D Objects** | **Wind Zone**). The **Palm_Desktop** tree was created in SpeedTree app, so it does not have this parameter available for it.

 Trees don't work with grouped objects. They will only use root GameObjects that have a Mesh Renderer component on them and ignore other objects down the hierarchy line.

Now that we have a tree in our palette, let's see what options are available to us:

Brush Size controls the area size in which trees will be created and with that increases the number of trees per stroke.

Tree Density controls the number of trees we can place on a single unit of a terrain. This is very handy as it prevents us from drawing over the same patch of trees and unintentionally increase its density.

The **Tree Height**, **Tree Width**, and **Color Variation** parameters, which you will see later, make trees more varied in height, width, and color. This allows the creation of a more natural feel to the forest. **Color Variation** shades some trees brighter and others darker. **Tree Height** and **Tree Width** are very useful parameters as well (width scales along **X** and **Z** axis).

The **Lock Width to Height** checkbox disables the **Tree Width** parameter and binds it to the **Tree Height** parameter.

The **Random** checkbox next to the **Tree Height** and **Tree Width** parameters will allow you to specify the range of tree scaling via a range slider (with **Random?** checked) or choose fixed scaling for all trees with an inputted number (with **Random?** unchecked).

Painting trees is very similar to anything else you've tried up to this point. The **Mass Place Trees** button will take all imported trees and distribute them on the terrain. By pressing the button, you will be able to specify the number of trees you want to be placed. Unity will distribute that number of trees among all the trees in your palette, and will place them on the terrain.

After placing trees, you can hold the *Shift* key to erase them where you don't need them, or hold the *Ctrl* key to erase the selected tree type only.

Let's get back to the **Enable Tree Collider** parameter (that was mentioned in the beginning of this chapter) in the **Terrain Collider** component. One of the common misconceptions about this parameter is that whenever it's checked, the trees will automatically get colliders. This is not so: only the trees that were created with a collider will have it activated. There could easily be thousands of trees in your level; calculating collision for all of them might be unnecessary and performance heavy. That's why you should keep track of those trees that have colliders and those that don't, and use them according to your needs. Otherwise, trees are well optimized in terms of performance thanks to the billboard technology they are based on; so you don't have to worry about having a lot of them in your scene.

 Whenever you modify your tree, do not forget to click on the **Refresh** button if you don't see the changes appearing on the screen.

Learning to use the Unity Tree editor

The Tree editor is a native Unity feature that enables the creation of any kind of tree as long as they have branches and something growing on them (usually leaves).

Before we start working with the Tree editor, make sure that you have the Environment package imported from **Assets | Import Package | Environment**. We will require some assets from it. We can create our first tree to work with from **GameObject | 3D Object | Tree**.

After selecting the tree and looking in the **Inspector** window, you will see a GameObject with a Tree component attached to it. This is where all the tools related to tree creation nest.

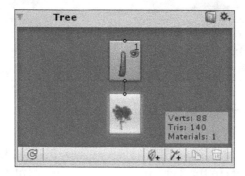

The tree creation feature is quite complex and contains a large amount of sliders, graphs, and parameters that will help you to adjust the tree to your liking. However, in this book, we will skip most of it and focus on the bare minimum of what you need to know in order to create your own tree in Unity.

The tree consists of three major components: a base (also known as tree **root node**), a branch (**branch group**), and a branch object (**leaf group**). The way they are structured is very intuitive: tree root node is at the base of the hierarchy; all other groups will be attached to it, or its children. Then, we have branch groups that can be parented to a tree root node or another branch group, allowing them to grow and split in multiple directions just like real trees do. On the top of branch groups, we can add leaf groups and adjust them to cover the area of that specific group in leaves.

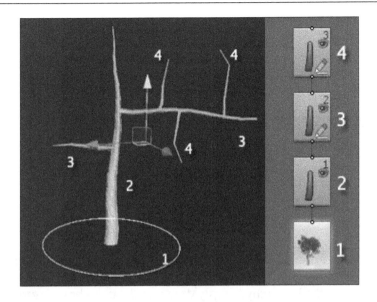

So there we go, that's how it works in theory. In Unity, whenever you create a new tree instance, it comes with a tree root node and a branch group as a default setup. The branch group here plays the role of a trunk. If you click on it in the **Inspector** window, you will notice that a tree gets highlighted and a trunk breaks down into multiple nodes in the **Scene** view. These nodes can be manipulated using Move Branch and Rotate Branch tools in the **Inspector** window. They can also be deleted by selecting and clicking on the *Delete* button on your keyboard, or created using the Free Hand tool. To use the Free Hand Tool, select a node and start drawing on your screen: new nodes will be created in set intervals.

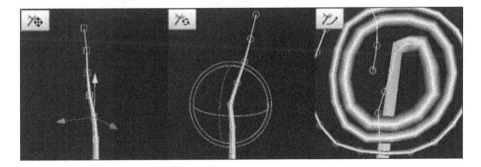

 Keep in mind that all the nodes that are above the node that you are drawing from, will be deleted automatically.

An important parameter of a branch group that you need to keep in mind, is **frequency**. It controls the number of branches created for each group. Just set this parameter to whichever number you want and adjust the newly created branches to your liking. Make sure you adjust this parameter before you go in and start manually adjusting branch position and length, otherwise it will become unavailable.

As stated earlier, you can have multiple branch groups with some complex hierarchy:

1. Select a Branch Group that you have in your Inspector window.

2. Click on the Add Branch Group button:

With a new branch group added, you can now adjust frequency and start removing branches wherever you don't need them. If you already have multiple branch groups and wish to change the hierarchy, simply drag and drop the branch group onto the one you wish to parent it to. Leaf groups work in a very similar manner.

To add a leaf group, select a branch group and click on Add Leaf Group.

Frequency is still your go-to parameter for controlling the number of leaves on each member of the branch group. Later, you can manually place the leaves with a mouse. Keep in mind that you can't detach a leaf from the branch it was created on.

Another interesting option worth mentioning is the **Geometry** mode for leaves. It allows you to change the representation of one leaf unit on your tree to one of the following:

*   **Plane**: This is the default mode in which a leaf will be represented with a single plane.

*   **Cross**: With this option, it will change to two planes being crossed.

*   **TriCross**: With this, you get three planes.

*   **Billboard**: This is a single plane that will always face the camera.

*   **Mesh**: This represents a leaf as a 3D mesh.

The last step is applying materials to our tree. As a bare minimum, we will require two materials: one for branches and one for leaves. To apply materials to the tree, follow these steps:

1. Go through each branch group in your tree editor and assign a **Tree_bark** material from the imported files, to the **Branch Material** property (under **Geometry** settings).

2. Do the same thing for each Leaf Group: assign the **Tree_leaves** material to the **Material** property (also under **Geometry**).

The leaf group is not only limited to actual leaves; you can also add fruits and any other kinds of detail.

One thing that you need to remember when creating your own materials for trees is that only those from the Nature category can be applied to branches or leaves.

Unity will issue a warning should the selected material type be inappropriate and will suggest changing the type by clicking on the **Apply** button. Naming conventions mentioned in the message are programming related — the actual material naming has no restrictions.

Now you can create a prefab and include your custom tree to the palette of your terrain and paint it.

This concludes our introduction to the Tree Creator. There are a lot more options available in there, and a lot more ways to control and customize your trees. If realistic trees are something you require in your project, I strongly recommend you explore this tool a little bit more.

With the recent addition of SpeedTree support for tree creation, you can now import vegetation created in the SpeedTree app into Unity. The **Palm_Desktop** tree that we used earlier was created using SpeedTree.

Paint details

Here is a tool that will allow you to truly enhance your environment.

What is considered a detail?

Details are generally referred to visual/non-interactive objects on the terrain, such as rocks, grass, flowers, mushrooms, etc.

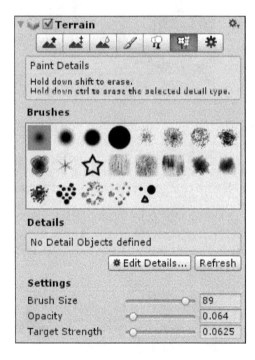

When I say noninteractive, I literally mean that there is no way to interact with them: they don't cast shadows or have collision detection.

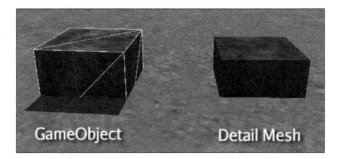

How to set up details

There are two variations of details according to Unity: Grass and Detail, which are essentially texture and mesh-based objects.

Grass

Let's start by creating a Grass type using texture based details.

1. Click on **Edit Details...** button.
2. Select **Add Grass Texture**.

This will open an option window for Grass detail.

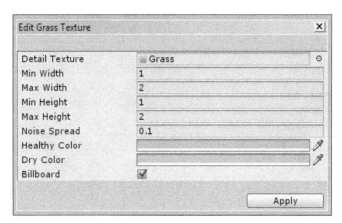

*   **Detail Texture** will be used for detail creation. For this example, we will use the **Grass1** texture from the `Chapter 3` folder.

- **Min/Max Width/Height** helps to diverse detail patches.
- **Noise Spread** controls the approximate size of the alternating patches; a higher parameter value will give you more variation within any given area.
- **Healthy/Dry Color** allows you to add color variation to the details.
- **Billboard** is a handy option, as it makes the detail (being a flat billboard) face the camera at all times, creating an illusion of density.

For custom textures to work, you'll need to create a texture with an alpha channel or transparency so that it will be rendered properly.

Details

Detail types or mesh-based details work in a similar way, but are created using 3D meshes.

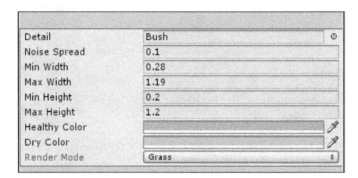

The settings here work in the same way as they do with the Grass details, except for the last parameter.

Render mode is a rendering method used on the detail object. There are only two to choose from: **Grass** and **VertexLit**. As a general rule, you should be using **Grass** on objects with textures that have alpha cutouts, such as bushes or flowers.

VertexLit, on the other hand, is perfect for solid objects, such as rocks, roots, and so on.

And that pretty much does it. Details certainly have their uses and can make your level look much better if used correctly. You will find more Detail assets to help with level creation within the Chapter 3 | Details folder. Put them to good use.

Customizing terrain settings

There are five categories available as options in the Terrain Settings tab:

- Base terrain
- Tree and detail objects
- Wind settings
- Resolution
- Heightmap

Each of them modifies their corresponding tools that we've looked at earlier.

We will avoid talking about Wind Setting and Wind Zones in general due to their limited application within Unity. However, here is what the other categories have to offer.

Base terrain

As you have probably guessed, this modifies properties of the terrain.

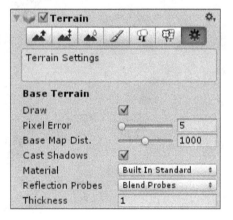

- **Draw** checkbox toggles terrain rendering.

- **Pixel Error** controls how accurately generated terrain will follow mapping; this parameter is essentially a tessellation for the terrain: the higher the value, the more polygons the terrain will use to represent applied mapping (height, textures…), and the faster it will lose polycount based on camera distance.

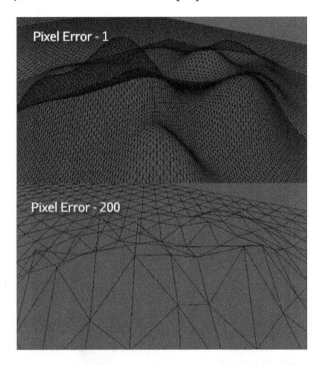

- **Base Map Distance** is a threshold at which terrain textures switch from full resolution to lower resolution.
- **Cast Shadows** enables/disables the shadows cast by the terrain.
- **Material** selects a material used by the terrain.
- **Reflection Probes** selects how the terrain will be affected by the reflection probes (this will only work if you are using Standard, or a custom material that supports reflection probes).
- **Thickness** helps to solve the issue of fast-moving physical objects penetrating the terrain by extending the terrain collision volume.

Tree and detail objects

Here are the settings for trees and details.

```
Tree & Detail Objects
Draw                            ☑
Bake Light Probes For Trees     ☑
Detail Distance         ──────○────────────  85
Collect Detail Patches          ☑
Detail Density          ────○──────────────  0.197
Tree Distance           ────────────────○──  2000
Billboard Start         ○──────────────────  50
Fade Length             ○──────────────────  5
Max Mesh Trees          ○──────────────────  50
```

The settings in the preceding screenshot are explained as follows:

- **Draw**: This enables us to draw trees, grass, and details.

- **Bake Light Probes for Trees**: This creates an individual light probe at the base of each tree as long as the base object has **Use Light Probes** checked in the Mesh Renderer component. If you've noticed the circles appearing around trees soon after placing them, those are the light probes. Don't worry, they will disappear in the **Game** window.

- **Detail Distance**: This is the camera culling distance for details.

- **Collect Detail Patches**: This allows you to preload all detail patches into memory to reduce hiccups.

- **Detail Density**: This increases the number of details/grass you can have in one area unit.

- **Tree Distance**: This is the camera culling distance for trees.

- **Billboard Start**: This is the distance from the camera at which 3D trees will be replaced with 2D billboards.

- **Fade Length**: This is the transition distance between 3D models and 2D billboards (this goes beyond the **Billboard Start** distance and pushes it further, by that number, as trees transition).

- **Max Mesh Trees**: This is the maximum number of trees that will be represented as 3D objects; others will be substituted with billboards.

Resolution

Resolution defines the size of the terrain, details, and heightmap.

Resolution	
Terrain Width	100
Terrain Length	100
Terrain Height	30
Heightmap Resolution	513
Detail Resolution	1024
Detail Resolution Per Patch	8
Control Texture Resolution	512
Base Texture Resolution	1024
* Please note that modifying the resolution will clear the heightmap, detail map or splatmap.	

The fields in the preceding screenshot are explained as follows:

- **Terrain Width/Length**: This is the size of the terrain (in world units).
- **Terrain Height**: This is the difference in height between the lowest and highest possible heightmap value in world units.
- **Heightmap Resolution**: This defines the resolution of a terrain heightmap (heightmap resolution of power of two + 1, 512+1=513 by default).
- **Detail Resolution**: This gives you smaller and more detailed patches of details and grass if its value is increased.
- **Detailed Resolution Per Patch**: This is the length/width of the square of patches rendered with a single draw call.
- **Control Texture Resolution**: This is splatmap resolution that controls blending between terrain textures.
- **Base Texture Resolution**: This is tied to Base Map Distance and specifies the resolution of textures used beyond the distance specified in Base Map Distance.

Skybox

Skybox can be a little bit more than just a pretty picture to cover the infinite void around our level; its properties can play a huge role in how our level is going to be lit:

1. Go to **Window | Lighting**.
2. In the **Scene** tab, under **Environment Lighting**, find the **Skybox** parameter.

Default-Skybox is a special material that exists in every Unity project and assigned as a default skybox. You can't edit, delete, or even find this material anywhere in the editor. However, you can replace it with your own custom skybox material.

To add a custom skybox, simply create a material and change its Shader type to **Skybox | Procedural**.

Now we have a new customizable Skybox that we can tweak and replace the default one with. Try to manipulate the sliders to set an interesting mood for your level, such as sunset or nighttime.

Summary

Oh boy! We really did cover a lot of ground with this one! All this work comes with the added benefit of you now being familiar with both the essential and situational tools needed to kick off the creation of any level. There are lots of things to be discovered about each of these tools, especially Water, Windzones, Skyboxes, and Tree Creation, that we've only scratched the surface of. Visit community forums if you have any specific questions or problems you can't find solutions to, and read the official documentation if you want in-depth technical information on how things work under the hood.

Sadly, while it is true that Unity doesn't always offer the best tools on the market for level creation, it does come with a large collection of user-created plugins and rich customization options that will allow you to push the power of Unity far ahead and get the tools that your team is looking for. The addition of SpeedTree app support and the ability to bring in custom terrains via heightmaps, will enable you to work with the tools of your liking.

In the next chapter, we will look into animations and how they are handled, imported, and even created in Unity.

4
Dealing with Basic Animations

This chapter describes how to create basic animations inside the Animation editor and import custom animations, to bring props in the level to life.

We will look into:

- Creation of custom animations in Unity
- Configuring animations
- Using Event Handlers to trigger function calls
- Importing animations into Unity

By the end of this chapter, you will become proficient with the basics of Unity's Legacy animation system.

Animation basics

Throughout its history, Unity has received a couple of features that deal with animations. In this chapter, we will talk about the oldest and simplest one. Unity Legacy Animation is a powerful feature that will help you to manage and set up imported animations. Its ability to create custom animations can prove to be invaluable during a prototyping phase. Though limited in options, it brings the benefit of simplicity and speed that attracts developers and causes them to rely on it, despite claims of the system being a thing of the past.

To follow the chapter's content, use the content from the Chapter 4 folder in your Project window. It contains objects that will be used in the future examples.

Using the Animation editor

The Unity Animation editor is fairly simple and limited; however, its main purpose is not to serve as a substitute for more sophisticated apps, but provide fast and easy solutions whenever you need to animate something simple.

Creating custom animations

Upon importing a mesh, we need to specify whether it has any animations that require importing. In case of `Windmill.fbx`, the one that we will use hereinafter, the answer will be, no; instead we will attempt to create our own custom animations using Unity's native editor.

For any other prop that does not have and/or does not intend to have any animations, it's a good habit to set the **Animation Type** parameter to **None** under the **Rig** tab of **Import Settings**.

The next recommended step is to create a prefab for the mesh before adding it into the scene.

We'll now focus on the GameObject that we will be animating; in this case, the Blade GameObject further down the Windmill hierarchy. In Unity, animations are stored inside animation clips that need to be assigned and stored in GameObject, in order to be accessed and played. To store these clips, GameObjects need to have an Animation component, under, **Add Component** | **Miscellaneous** | **Animation**.

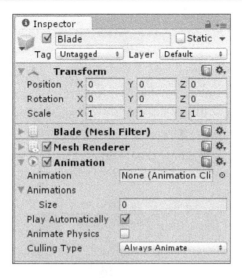

Add this component to the Blade GameObject. What this does is allow us to add and store animation clips.

- **Animation**: This is the first animation clip that will be played by default, if specified.

- **Animations**: This is an array of all available animations for a current GameObject.

- **Play Automatically**: This is a flag that plays the animation specified in the **Animation** property, whenever the game starts (or whenever the object is created in the scene).

- **Animate Physics**: This checks whether the animation should interact with physics.

- **Culling Type**: This includes two options—**Always Animate** and **Based On Renderers**. The first one will always animate; the second one, however, will only play the animation if the object is rendered by the camera (which is useful if you want some extra optimization).

So how are the actual animations created?

To discover that, we need to go to **Window | Animation** from the menu bar; this will open an Animation editor.

Editor controls

As you can see there aren't that many options and we can easily discuss them as we go.

You can only use this tool on GameObjects in the scene. Therefore, our newly created prefab for the Windmill object has to be dragged into the scene in order to be animated.

With the object in place, we can now create an animation by clicking on the **Clip** drop-down menu, that appears to be empty by default, and selecting the **Create New Clip** option.

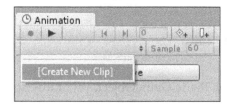

Create a folder called Animations inside the Chapter 4 folder and name the clip Windmill_BladeSpin.

Our clip is now available under the **Animation** drop-down menu and can be edited.

To start animating, we click on the **Add Curve** button underneath the **Animation** menu and select a component and a property that we wish to animate. In this case, we will be navigating to **Transform | Rotation**.

With the curve added, you will not only notice that keyframes appear along the Dope Sheet, but the recording button turns red (the red dot sign), and the **Rotation** property changes color in the **Inspector** window.

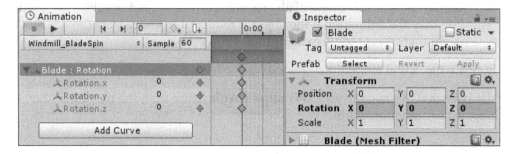

This indicates to us that any changes to our object will be recorded at a specified point on the timeline.

Let's create the actual animation by:

1. Selecting the last keyframe on the Dope Sheet (the top most).

2. Rotating the Blade GameObject in the scene view, a full 360 degrees clockwise or counterclockwise.

3. Clicking on the play button in the **Animation** window

The GameObject should now be playing the animation in the scene window. You can also manually input the values into the Animation window; however, keep in mind that these values utilize, not the default Centered Pivot, but the native Pivot of the object.

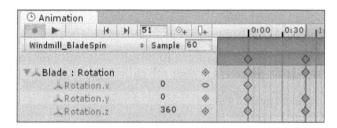

There are few other things worth mentioning before we move on. Keyframes can be created automatically by clicking at any point on the timeline, and modifying the selected property of the object. Alternatively, you can use an Add Keyframe button ( ). Keyframes can be deleted by selecting them and pressing the *Delete* key on your keyboard.

Keyframes can be moved by dragging them along the timeline. You might notice that you can't actually move different rotation axes independently, but need to move an entire rotation property as a whole. This has to do with the fact that these variables are set to read only, while the rotation component can be rewritten.

The **Sample** property specifies frames per second and it could be useful to change this, if you require more control over quick animations. Keep in mind that this will not change the play speed of the animation in the scene window. The biggest inconvenience with Animation component is that animation clips that are assigned to it will not be played in the Play mode of Unity 5, unless they are marked as Legacy. We can easily fix this by:

1. Selecting the **Windmill_BladeSpin** animation clip in the **Project** window

2. Clicking on the drop down menu of the **Inspector** window in the top right corner and selecting **Debug** option

3. Checking **Legacy** box

After completing this procedure you can return Inspector window to the Normal mode and assign Windmill_BladeSpin to the Animation parameter of the Animation component to see it being played upon entering Play mode. Make sure to do the same thing to every clip you assign to the Animation component.

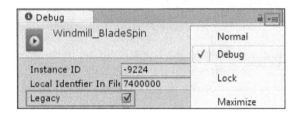

The Curve editor

Dope Sheet is not the only tool we can use to modify our animations. At the bottom of the Animation window, there is another tab called **Curves** that will take us to the Curve editor.

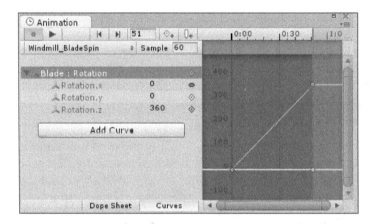

To make the curves fit the screen, simply select the Rotation property and then hit the *F* key on the keyboard while hovering over the right side of the window with the mouse cursor.

If you have any experience in animation, using this tool should come naturally to you.

Keyframes are being connected by lines that represent the interpolation of the parameter on the timeline known as **Curves**. Each keyframe (apart from borderline right and left) has two tangents that allow them to modify the curves on both of their sides.

The best way to understand this is by trying to do it yourself with the following steps:

1. Start off by creating a new keyframe by right-clicking along the **Rotation.z** curve and clicking on **Add Key**.

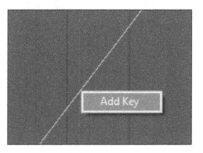

2. Now right-click on the newly created keyframe.

You will see a number of options displayed:

- ○ **Delete Key**: This will simply delete the keyframe
- ○ **Auto**: This is a mode that will attempt to smooth out the tangents on both sides to make the curve look smooth
- ○ **Free Smooth**: This will make the tangents visible and you will be able to manually adjust them

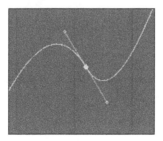

- ○ **Flat**: This will move tangents to a horizontal position

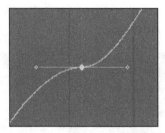

- ○ **Broken**: This will allow you to adjust tangents independently, giving more control, however, sacrificing the smooth look

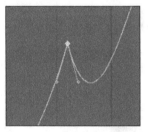

- ○ **Left Tangent**, **Right Tangent**, and **Both Tangents**: These allow you to select one of the three modes for tangents of this keyframe
- ○ **Free**: This is a current default mode
- ○ **Linear**: This will force linear interpolation between keyframes
- ○ **Constant**: This will remove interpolation entirely

That's about it for the editor. Since the Animation editor is primarily made to deal with rough animations for prototyping, you will find yourself using Dope Sheet to create keyframes and only going into the Curve editor to adjust it slightly or fix a weird animation behavior.

Give it a try

Try to practice with the curve tool by creating new keyframes and adjusting curves so as to change the rotation speed of the blades. Make it look like the blades received a powerful impulse and quickly reached the maximum rotation speed. After that, make it slow down before reaching a complete stop. Here are the steps:

1. Start from a complete stop.

2. Rapidly increase the rotation speed while at the same time decrease the acceleration before the animation reaches one third of its length.

3. Gradually, slow the rotation down before it reaches a complete stop.

4. Make sure that there are no jumps in animation when looping (last and first frames need to have blades in a similar position, not necessarily rotation).

Did it work? Trying to make the last frame identical to the first one should have been problematic, since you shouldn't end up at zero rotations at the end of the animation.

Custom animations and world space

Let's try to animate the root of the windmill GameObject to shift right and left. Nothing big, just simple movement and make sure to add the Animation component and mark clip as Legacy in Debug mode. When you're done, try this: move the original location of the object and see how the animation responds to it in the scene view. The animation does not care where the object stood initially, it will always animate it using specified values relative to the world space.

But what about the blades we animated earlier? By removing the windmill shifting animation, and moving the windmill around, we should see that the blades always rotate properly in their set position. That is because the blades were animated within a local space of their parent object; therefore, they're relative to it. The windmill shifting animation can easily be fixed if we parent it to an empty GameObject (**GameObject | Empty GameObject**) and animate it that way; this is a common trick that can be used with any animation since it's always relative to something.

Triggering the event handlers with animation

Event handlers are a very cool feature that allow you to call functions also known as events from the scripts attached to the animated GameObject. This is very useful and can save a lot of time if you need something to happen at a certain point of the animation.

To showcase this functionality, we will use our Windmill GameObject by performing these steps:

1. Select the **Blade** GameObject of the Windmill that we've animated earlier.

2. Attach a Box Collider component to it (**Physics | Box Collider**).

3. Attach a script file called `WindmillMessage.cs` inside `Chapter 4` folder to the **Blade** GameObject.

4. Uncheck the **Play Automatically** parameter in the Animation component.

5. Position the MainCamera in the scene view to look directly at the Windmill (you should see a Windmill in the Game window).

Attaching a Box Collider is not necessary for events that are called from the animation. The script is coded to start the `Windmill_BladeSpin` animation that we created earlier, upon clicking on the Blade (the actual click cannot be registered without the collider).

Now we can go into the Animation editor and set up the event call by performing the following steps:

1. Select the last keyframe and click on the **Add Event** Button.

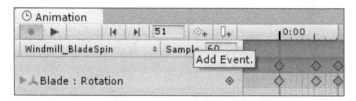

2. In the new window, select **EventFunction()** (this is the name of the function within the script).

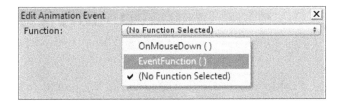

3. That should be it; in the last frame, you should see an event sign appear.

Now, whenever you start the game and click on the Windmill with the left mouse button, the windmill will turn white at the end of the animation.

Scripts, like any other components, can be modified with the Animation editor; for instance, you can change the variable values just like we did with rotation to create a `Windmill_BladeSpin` animation.

Importing the prop animation into Unity

Now that custom animations are done with, let's see how to import actual animations created with other apps along with a mesh.

Inside the `Chapter 4` folder, there are two models; let's take a look at the other one: **Chest.fbx**.

Since this mesh inherently has animations attached to it, we need to specify that in the import settings by selecting **Legacy** for the **Animation Type** parameter under the **Rig** tab. Doing this will also mark all it's animation clips as Legacy.

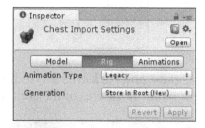

We will talk about other animation types in future chapters when we look at another animation system this is also available in Unity.

Now we'll move on to the next tab, **Animations**. This tab can be divided into three sections dubbed: general settings, clip settings, and clip preview.

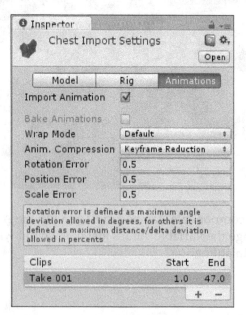

General Settings are at the very top; they provide some basic animation settings for this mesh and contain a list of clips drawn from the animation timeline. The settings in the preceding screenshot are explained as follows:

- **Import Animation**: This is a checkbox that should always be checked if you plan to use the object's animations.
- **Bake Animations**: This is a little trickier. This this will only be available for Maya, 3DsMax, and Cinema4D files and allows us to use IK handles or simulation in our animation package. Suffice to say that this FBX object does not belong to any of the apps mentioned earlier and doesn't contain any IK handles or simulation, which is why this option is unavailable.
- **Wrap Mode**: This specifies a default wrap mode for the animations on their import, which can later be changed with scripts at runtime, or manually for each Animation clip.

Here is the list of animation wrap modes available in Unity:

- **Default**: This will use options specified in any individual clip
- **Once**: This will play an animation clip once and then stop
- **Loop**: This will play animation over and over again resetting upon reaching the end
- **Ping Pong**: This plays animation back and forth reversing each time it reaches the end
- **Clamp Forever**: This will play animation until the end and continue to repeat the last frame indefinitely (unlike the Once mode, it doesn't stop)

- **Anim. Compression** will try to reduce the number of keyframes in your animation on import to increase performance and reduce the animation size.
    - If you want 100 percent accurate animation to be played, try turning this option **Off**
    - If you value optimization more with, the additional benefit of control over the optimization options: **Keyframe Reduction** mode is your choice
    - If you are also concerned about the size of your project (which is very common for mobile devices), try the last **Keyframe Reduction and Compression** mode which will include benefits of the previous mode as well.

Selecting either of the two latter options will enable three parameters control over keyframe reduction in terms of rotation, position, and scale. Numbers themselves don't say much about how the animation will be changed; however, they are still important to understand should any issues occur or if you are trying to see how far you can push the keyframe reduction.

- **Rotation error**: This defines the minimum difference in rotation values (in degrees) below which, two keyframes are counted as equals.

- **Position error**: This is the minimum difference in position (as a percentage of coordinate values) below which, two keyframes are counted as equal.

- **Scale error**: This is the minimum difference in scale (as a percentage of coordinate values) below which, two keyframes are counted as equal.

Based on these statements, we can assume that the higher these values are set, the higher the keyframe reduction will be.

There is no telling which values are best to use, since it's all based on the animation; however, it would be best to test your animation without keyframe reduction first, make sure that everything is working fine and then apply and tweak it to suit your needs. This will greatly reduce your frustration level when something goes wrong.

Clips is a list of animation slices from the animation timeline. If all of your animation is on a single timeline, this allows you to manually slice it into multiple clips.

Our current object has two animations—one for the locked state, when a player tries to open a chest without a key, and the other for an opening state, when a player opens it with a key. Click on the plus sign to add a new clip.

The following animation settings are clip settings that modify each individual clip selected in the clips listed earlier:

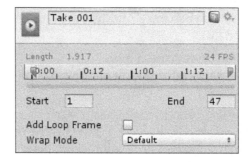

The name of our first clip is **Take 001**; it's a default name given to the first unnamed clip.

 Curiously enough, our second clip is called **Take 0010**; however, any consecutive clips' number will only be incremented by 1, not 9 (**Take 0011, Take 0012**…).

Below the name field, there is a timeline that shows the length of a clip segment, the frame rate at which it has been recorded, and the borders that can be dragged to manually adjust the clip's segment location on a timeline and its length. You can also specify the borders in the **Start** and **End** fields. The settings in the preceding screenshot are explained as follows:

- **Add Loop Frame**: This tries to smooth animation slightly by adding an extra frame at the end that is identical to the first frame. However, this could make some animations look weird.
- **Wrap mode**: This allows us to specify a wrap mode for this particular clip.

Let's use these options to slice and set up, both of our animations. For the first clip, perform the following steps:

1. Select the `Take 001` clip in the clips list and name it `Locked`.
2. Set the **Start** frame to **1** and **End** to **24**.
3. Change **Wrap Mode** to **Once**.

For the second clip, set the following parameters:

1. Click on the plus sign under the Clips list, if you haven't before, and select the newly created clip in the Clips list.
2. Name it `Opening`.
3. Set **Start** to **24** and **End** to **40**.
4. Change **Wrap Mode** to **Clamp Forever**.
5. Click on the **Apply** button.

You can now play these animations in the Clip Preview window at the bottom of the import settings. Just select the clip you wish to see and hit the play button.

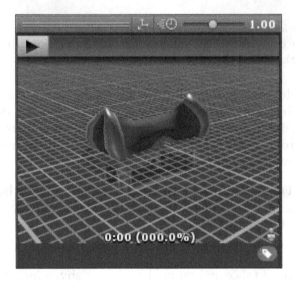

If you can't see the object in the Preview window or the object displayed is not a chest, just perform the following steps:

1. Click on the icon at the bottom-left corner.
2. Select **Other....**.
3. Find and select a Chest mesh in the Object Picker window.

Done! You can now create a prefab for the model and drag a Chest into the scene. You will notice in your Inspector view that animations are already included into the Animation Component.

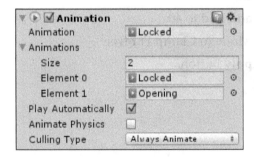

Adding custom animations will be tempting, and it is possible. To do this, you need to increment a **Size** parameter of the **Animations** array and leave it blank. This way, an option to create a new animation clip in the Animation window will become available.

However, you cannot modify imported animations via this editor, they are read only.

The chest was not animated with IK handles or bones, but simply setting keyframes along the timeline in a 3D app. Importing prop animations into Unity should not pose any problem; simply perform the following steps:

1. Animate the prop with keyframes.
2. Export the mesh with animations in .fbx (or any other format you prefer).
3. Slice the animation into clips inside Unity.

We will look into bones and IK handles when we talk about character animations.

Summary

The animation type that we've looked at in this chapter is called Legacy animation. Before the release of Unity 4, it was the only way to work with animations in Unity; however, despite the fact that we now have a much more advanced and flexible Mecanim system, a lot of people are still using the old school version for its simplicity and ability to create custom animations within Unity. The sad news is that Unity developers confirmed that, over time, they will try to get rid of Legacy animation for good, and only keep it for the sake of backward compatibility. However, before that happens, Legacy Animation is the only tool that will allow you to create animations inside Unity.

In the next chapter, we will look into the character import pipeline and also how to use Mecanim to set up animations.

5
Invite Your Characters to Unity

This chapter is all about taking your modeled, rigged, and animated characters from your 3D modeling software and importing them into Unity.

In this chapter, we'll cover the following topics:

- Exporting character models from a 3D software package
- Configuring generic and humanoid animation types
- Creating a character avatar
- Getting your character ready for the Mecanim

By the end of this chapter, you will learn about the character import process, its benefits, and how to deal with any issues. The example in this book features a specific 3D modeling software package; however, even though the steps might differ, the general process is the same, no matter what you choose to go with.

Get your character ready

I have to tell you—the way you go about rigging and animating your character can, and most likely will, vary from the example shown here. It may depend on the software you are using, your needs, or your devotion to certain standards. That being said, most paths will allow you to bake animations and export them in the .fbx format. You don't have to do that though! If the Unity supports the native file extension of your software of choice (at the moment Unity recognizes the 3D Max, Maya, and Blender file formats) you should be able to import it as is and use it in Unity (I am personally not familiar with every software program there is for animation so I can't say for sure that you won't encounter any problems along the way). However, by baking animations and exporting them in more or less generic formats, we will be able to get on the same page regardless of where we've started from.

Exporting from Blender

Our character is fully modeled, rigged, skinned, and animated in Blender.

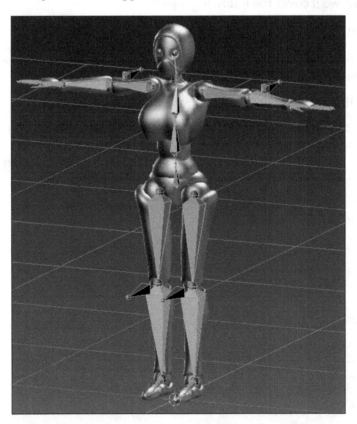

Model overview

This file contains all of the information about our character, there are no references of any kind, and all animations are done on a single timeline.

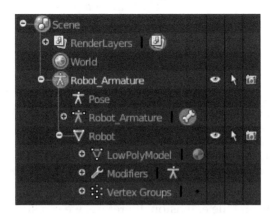

The file is named `Robot.fbx` and can be found inside the `Chapter 5` folder of the complimentary files.

Apart from the geometry and the skeleton, it also contains a pair of IK handles for legs and arms. In the end, we have a very basic character ready to be used for video games. You can try to challenge yourself and bring a high-poly model with a fancy rig and a complex set of animations, but that will only equate to doing extra tweaking in Unity further down the line and there are certain limitations posed by Unity that will encourage you to keep it as optimal as possible.

Let's talk about the skeleton. In order for your character to be working in Unity, you don't have to go out of your way and force a certain bone topology. However, if you are building a humanoid, it should have a bone topology similar to humanoids—no three legged/ four armed creatures can actually be considered humanoids by Unity standards, but can still be imported and used.

The skeleton structure of our character is not a template by any stretch of the imagination and you don't have to follow it; work with what you feel comfortable with and I'll show you how to communicate your preference to Unity later in this chapter.

Exporting as FBX

In this section we are going to look into how to export the character into FBX using Blender, a `.blend` file can be found in the same folder as the `Robot.fbx`. This character is ready to be exported. There are a few general things to consider before we get it into Unity:

- Character stands solidly on the ground at 0,0,0 coordinates
- Character is scaled properly
- Check your T-pose to make sure that the palms are facing the ground
- Check your normals to make sure they are facing the right direction

 1 Unity unit equals to 1 meter; for better optimization and smoother import make sure to scale your character in the 3D app, accordingly.

Unity supports the `.blend` file extension; therefore, we can simply import it directly or export it to the `.fbx` file format in the following manner:

1. In Blender, navigate to **File** | **Export** | **FBX** (**Import-Export:FBX** format add-on needs to be enabled).
2. In the options, check the **Baked Animation** box.
3. Hit **Export**.

Your file can now be safely imported into Unity.

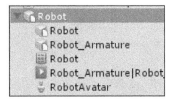

You don't have to get rid of curve controls after baking animations for exporting; they won't cause any problems and won't be visible in the game.

Importing referenced animations

For those of you who use referenced animations—Unity's got you covered.

Here is another example of a file that is referencing a different file that contains geometry and rig, but no animations. This reference file, on the other hand, contains our arm animation and a reference, nothing more. This is a different character and this time in Maya.

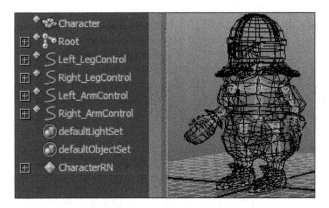

Here is the process of getting this animation into Unity assuming that you've already imported your referenced model in the .fbx format:

1. Bake animation by navigating to **Edit | Keys | Bake simulation**.
2. Select character's entire skeleton (every node).
3. Export that in .fbx format by going **File | Export Selected** (you'll only need your skeleton, nothing else).
4. Name the file Character_animationPass@ArmAnim.fbx.

5. Import that into Unity, in the same folder as the referenced model.

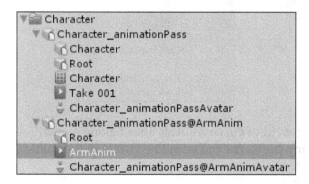

Unity will automatically assign the referenced model to the animation and will allow us to use it with our character.

The key here is the file referencing the model, and the correct naming convention for the animation file, which should be as follows: `referencename@animationname.` `fbx`. In this case, our original file was named **Character_animationPass** and then we named our animation **ArmAnim**, which you will see in the hierarchy window in Unity.

Rinse and repeat for other animations if that is your usual working pipeline. The major benefit of this approach is being able to add as many animations as you like after importing the model into Unity.

We've covered the basics behind the character export from one of the 3D applications, but there are others with their unique nuances. To find out how to export from a specific 3D app, visit the Unity official documentation, where you can read about importing objects from a specific app at:

`http://docs.unity3d.com/Manual/HOWTO-importObject.html`.

If you are using Blender and Rigify for character rigging, the following article on how to import a Rigify rig into Unity should interest you:

`http://docs.unity3d.com/Manual/BlenderAndRigify.html`.

Configuring a character in Unity

We will continue working with the character that was imported with embedded animations.

With the character imported, we go right to the **Rig** tab of **Import Settings** to explore the remaining two animation types: **Generic** and **Humanoid**. As mentioned in previous chapters, there are two animation types that are required in order to use Mecanim, a powerful animation control tool introduced in the 4th version of Unity. I can't stress enough, how awesome Mecanim is; this system allows you to significantly improve your development pipeline and reduce the amount of code to control animations, but more about that in the next chapter. Right now we need to figure out how to set up the model to be used by this system.

Generic and humanoid – what's the difference?

This is exactly how it sounds—Generic can be used for everything, from a dragon to a toaster, whereas, Humanoid can only be used on the characters that have the humanoid bone topology.

Generic Animation Type

Generic is the easier type and you might end up using and relying on it most of the time especially when the humanoid doesn't work for you. So let's get the easier part out of the way and look at the following:

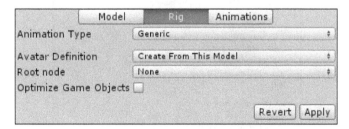

- **Avatar Definition**: **Generic Animation Type** doesn't allow us to make full use of **Character Avatar**, so leave it at the default; as **Create From This Model.**

- **Root node**: This is the node that contains animation translation; by selecting the node from the drop-down menu, you will enable the **Root Motion** parameters in the **Animation** tab. For now set **Root node** to **Robot** from the drop down menu.

- **Optimize Game Objects**: By default, Unity creates an empty GameObject for every transform in your character, checking this box allows us to prevent this from happening and increase the overall performance, since Unity doesn't have to deal with those extra transforms.

Thankfully, you can still create some of these transforms on demand if you need to reference them through the code. Select the transform from the hierarchy by clicking on the **+** sign of the **Extra Transforms to Expose** list which appears when you've selected the **Optimize Game Objects** option.

Now let's move to the **Animation** tab and look at how the **Clip** options changed since we last used them for **Legacy Animation**.

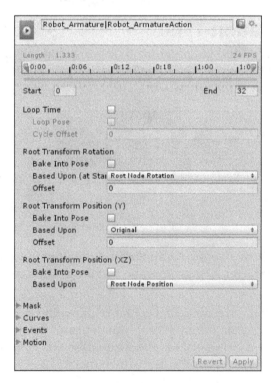

As you can see, there is a significant increase in the number of options, as follows:

- **Loop Time**: Checking this option will make our clip play through till the end and then restart from the beginning. This also enables the following options:

    ° **Loop Pose**: This makes your animation loop seamlessly. However, this only works well if the starting pose matches the end pose; it will take the difference and will make a blend throughout the clips length to make them match.

    ° **Cycle Offset**: This is the offset to the cycle of a looping animation.

- **Root Transform Rotation, Root Transform Position (Y),** and **Root Transform Position (XZ)**: These serve a very similar purpose — they prevent the GameObject from being rotated or translated along the respected axis by the AnimationClip. In other words, if you don't want your GameObject to be moved by the animation, check **Bake Into Pose** in the required category, to prevent it. They will only appear if you've specified the **Root Node** in the **Rig** tab.

- **Based Upon**: You can choose the GameObjects rotation or position to be based on the **Root Node** specified in the **Rig** tab, or the way you set it up on exporting, by choosing **Original**.

- **Offset**: This allows you to add the offset to the rotation or translation of the GameObject if you chose **Root Transform Rotation** or **Root Transform Position (Y)** to be based on **Root Node** (the **Original** values will be taken from the model).

- **Mask**: This is very simple to understand and use. Let's say you need to remove a motion from the **Neck** transform, and its children, in one of your animations. To do that you, need to go under the **transform** menu, and uncheck the **Neck** transform. If you run the animation now, you will notice that the **Neck** transform, and its children, aren't moving. We will talk about the application of Masks in the next chapter.

- **Definition**: This allows you to choose to, either create the mask from this specific model, or copy it from another mask.

To create a custom avatar mask for our character, do the following:

1. Click on **Create** from the drop down menu and select **Avatar Mask**.

2. Go under the **Transform** drop down menu of the **Avatar Mask**.

3. Drag the **RobotAvatar** generated by our character model (it can be found inside the imported **Robot** model).

4. Click on the **Import skeleton** button.

This should load all the transforms from our character, into the mask, and allow us to configure them here, to be assigned to multiple objects with the same bone structure.

Events are improved and expanded from the Legacy Animation; now you can trigger any function on any GameObject just by filling in the blanks and specifying the frame on the timeline.

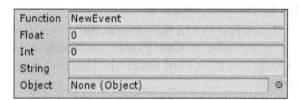

This covers the **Animation** tab for the **Generic Animation Type**; we will omit talking about the **Curves** and **Motion** parameters as they aren't required for this example.

Humanoid Animation Type

Imagine yourself in a situation where you have multiple humanoid characters that require the same animation — sitting, walking, running, and so on; or there is a specific animation that you would like to reuse on multiple humanoids. Usually, you would be required to create each animation for every single character, taking into consideration their body proportions. With **Humanoid Animation Type**, that is not the case, you can cut out a lot of steps in your usual animation pipeline by referencing animations using **CharacterAvatars**, and tweak them to match and tailor to any character using a muscle system. Let's take a look at how this is done.

Character avatar

First things first, we need to switch our **Animation Type** of the imported Robot from **Generic** to **Humanoid**, and hit **Apply**.

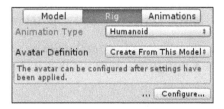

Avatar Definition, using the default **Create From This Model** parameter, will generate a Robot Avatar for this model automatically, by trying to map the Robot's skeleton onto the humanoid topology. The key factors in successful mapping are hierarchy and naming (bone direction and ratio also contribute, however, not as significantly as those two). The algorithm will search for a bone called **Hip**, check if it's a root bone, and which bones are attached to it. So make sure that you're using proper naming conventions to get the best out of this process.

If the process is successful you'll see a check mark next to the **Configure...** button, but regardless, let's click on it and see what has actually happened.

Unity will open a new scene with our character in the center and ask you to save the current scene; it would be wise to do so.

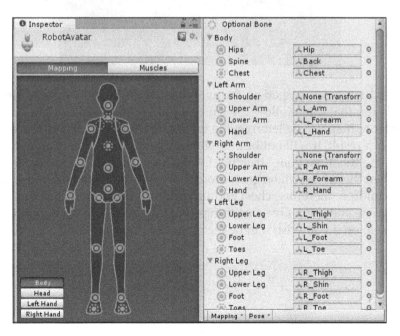

Robot Avatar shows us a humanoid body with bones represented by lined (mandatory) and dotted (optional) circles. As you can see, all the mandatory bones were successfully matched, leaving a few optional bones unchecked.

We can check the rest of our bones by switching between body parts at the right bottom corner (**Body**, **Head**, **LeftHand**, and **RightHand**).

Here is where it gets interesting. Take a look at the **Scene** window in our character model (hitting the **Configure...** button takes us to a different scene with our character).

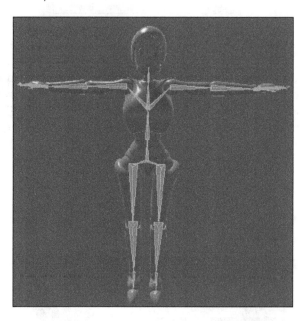

All the bones that were mapped on the avatar successfully, now appear green. Any additional bones that don't follow the Unity topology standards will be marked as grey. In order to map the skeleton on the template, Unity will exclude any additional bones and, as a result, it will not be animated. A very common example of this is, if you are using the three bone structure for the torso such as the lower back, spine, and chest, then the spine will be grayed out; however, unlike avatar mask, it doesn't exclude its children, therefore, chest and its children will animate just fine. This is a bit unfortunate and there are some things that you need to keep in mind when creating a skeleton if you wish it to be recognized as a humanoid by Unity.

Correct topology

By topology, I mean that the skeleton must have certain bones that follow a strict hierarchy. Now, that doesn't mean that your character must have a certain skeleton or bust, you may or may not have certain bones, but there are those that define us as humanoids and they must exist. Here is the structure skeleton we must respect in order for our character to be recognized as a humanoid by Unity standards:

- **Hips | Upper Leg | Lower Leg | Foot | Toes**
- **Hips | Spine | Chest | Neck | Head**
- **Chest | Shoulder | Arm | Forearm | Hand**
- **Hand | Proximal | Intermediate | Distal**

The sad part here is that if you have any extra bones that are not included in the list, there is no way to add them to the avatar, the list is fixed. Keep in mind, however, that the humanoid animation type was designed as a compromise based on numerous humanoid rig standards. If you are using a different standard or have more bones to increase control and precision, or using the humanoid rig screws in your animation, then you can always switch to **Generic** without a need to re-rig your character.

Wrong topology example

Allow me to illustrate an example how a perfectly fine bone structure created in Blender can go wrong when viewed in Unity.

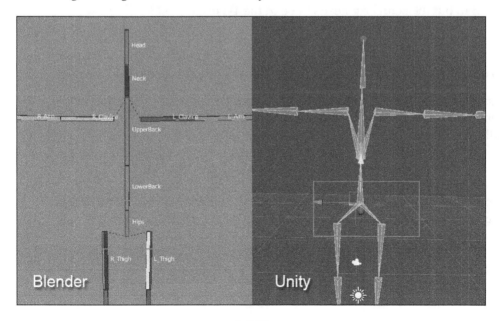

If you look at the image above you'll see that the **Hips** bone is the only one grayed out by Unity. That is happening because **Hips** is a child of the **LowerBack** bone. This is where Unity gets confused; it automatically assigns the topmost bone in the hierarchy to be **Hips**, searches down the hierarchy for two bones that represent **UpperLegs** and finds **R_Thigh** and **L_Thigh** (since they are children of the **LowerBack** child bone, they meet the requirements and will work just fine). But with our **Hips** bone from Blender, Unity will simply ignore it, as well as the animation data associated with it, as if it doesn't exist.

If you aren't planning on using animation referencing, you may simply ignore this issue and switch to **Generic Animation Type**, everything is going to work just fine there. However, if you do plan to rely on the animation referencing, then the only way to make it work, will be to go back to Blender, and reparent bones so that **LowerBack** is a child of the **Hips** bone.

Muscles

Before we go into this topic, there is one thing that is vital to proper muscle work, and that is the T-pose. Make sure that your character was modeled and rigged in the T-pose; this is very important. If, for any reason, that's not the case with your character, you can follow these steps:

1. Find the **Pose** drop down menu at the bottom of the **Inspector** window
2. Select **Enforce T-Pose**

With a bit of luck, this will help (note that it's OK to have your character animated out of it, but the actual rig needs to be in the T-Pose).

The actual muscles in Unity are deceptively easy to use. Think of them as restrains that you might have already applied during the rigging process. Unity tries to apply its own settings of how the body parts should bend and twist.

Let's talk about the benefits of it. Imagine that you have an animation that is to be applied on two characters, one of which is naked and the other one is geared in full plate medieval armor. Simply referencing animation won't work, you would have a naked character looking stiff, or geared with body parts penetrating his own armor. Muscles allow you to configure their avatars individually, applying different restrains and making sure that the animations look better on both of them. Don't expect this system to create miracles and make a full plated guy's backflip look equally pretty, as it is ridiculous (unless you've designed a specific armor set).

As for the actual muscle configuration, it's very intuitive:

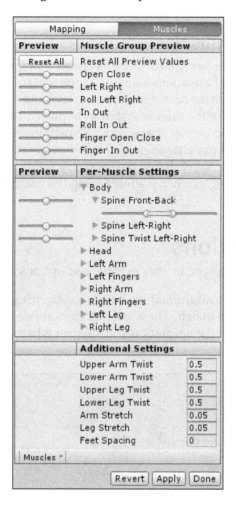

The editor is divided into three categories:

- **Muscle Group Preview**: This allows you to test a group of muscles by applying different motions that may or may not be a part of your animation.

- **Per-Muscle Settings**: This allows you to apply restrains on each individual muscle (generated from a humanoid skeleton and mapped on a character's bones). You can dig into hierarchy, specify the range of motion using the slider on the right, and test it with a slider on the left, under a **Preview** column.

- **Additional Settings**: This gives you extra options to play with to make sure that your character animates well.

After all the options are set, just click on **Apply**, then on the **Done** button, and you will return to the previous scene.

Adjust character muscles

In the next chapter, we will be importing the locomotion animation package from the Unity Asset Store. The Humanoid animation type will help us to reference them onto our character, but to make sure that the character looks fine with a random set of animations; proper set up of the muscle system is required. Try to edit the muscles and utilize the motion sliders to restrict character movement in order to avoid geometry overlapping. In the case of our character, the most problematic area will be the chest that might cause the hands to crush into the geometry while running. The final result should have no overlapping geometry while testing the character with the **Muscle Group Preview** sliders.

Additional options

The Humanoid animation type further extends our options in the **Animation** tab.

Animation clips now have additional indicators for **Looping**, **RootTransforms**, and **Root Rotation** called **loop match**. These indicators evaluate the difference between the first and final frame of the animation and suggest whether the **Loop Pose** option should be used.

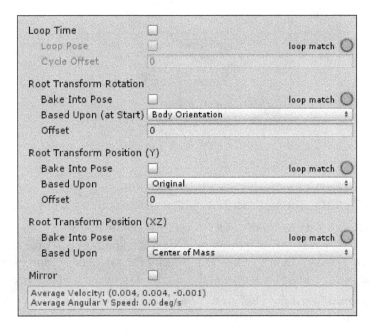

The new humanoid animation type also brought a **Humanoid** setting to a **Mask**.

Using the humanoid mask, you can enable or disable the different groups of muscles and IKs to be affected by the animation, and see the result right in the preview window. As of v5.01, Unity supports only **LeftFoot**, **RightFoot**, **LeftHand**, and **RightHand** IK goals for the humanoid animation type.

This concludes this part of the animation pipeline. I hope you've managed to grasp the essentials of how this system works and what to expect from it.

Summary

Getting your characters from the 3D modeling software to Unity could not have been easier. Unity's support of popular file formats and additional compatibility with Blender, Maya, and 3Ds Max creates a very flexible pipeline. Humanoid animation type is an amazing feature that can speed up your animation process if you are willing to adjust to its strict standards.

If you still experience strange behavior with your rig after importing it into Unity, try searching the Unity forums (`http://forum.unity3d.com/`) for solutions, chances are other people have experienced the same problem and managed to find a solution to it.

In the following chapter, we will finally take a good look at this new beast called Mecanim and see how far we can get with all the work we've done up until now.

6
Using Mecanim for Advanced Animations

The Mecanim animation system is a major feature of the 4th version of Unity. It's flexible and easy to use, with the additional benefits of reducing programmer involvement in building animation systems and shortening the development cycle in general. This is the part where you'll learn why that is the case.

Throughout the chapter, we will look into the following topics:

- The animator tool's basics and functionalities
- Creation and control of state machines
- Blending, combining, and layering motions
- Creating basic locomotion

By the end of this chapter, you will be able to setup, control, and maintain animation systems in a matter of minutes with minimum reliance on coding. We will look into different case scenarios based on available animations, functionality requirements, and rigs. Without further ado, let's get started!

The animator controller

Animation control is a tedious and complicated process. Mandatory proficiency in programming for all developers who used the **Legacy** animation system pretty much resulted in animation control being fully delegated to programmers writing state machine codes. Well, that's not the case anymore. A little bit of coding is still required, however, it plays more of a support role since major work is now done in Visual Editor, which allows animators to take full control of how and when animations are played, setup transitions, limitations, and control them with conditions. This new system is known as Mecanim.

To avoid skepticism, I will stop singing the praises of the system itself and give you a hands-on experience of how it really works.

But before we do that, there are a few things we need to take care of:

1. Create a prefab for the Robot and drag it into the scene.

2. Open **Asset Store** by navigating to **Window | Asset Store** in the menu on top of the screen.

3. Type **Raw mocap data for Mecanim** in the search field.

4. Select **Raw mocap data for Mecanim** from the search result.

5. Click on the **Import** button to download the package.

This package is provided for free by **Unity Technologies**.

If we click on our robot's prefab right now we will see that it has a component attached to it called Animator. That's the Mecanim version of the Animation component for the Legacy system. However, unlike Animation, it doesn't store a list of clips; instead, it holds state machines in an Animator Controller object. In order to work with Mecanim, we need to create an object:

1. Click on **Create** in the **Project** window.
2. Select **Animator Controller**.
3. Name it **CharacterController**.
4. Assign it to the **Controller** parameter of the **Animator** component.
5. Make sure that **Apply Root Motion** is checked.

Animation states

Double-click on the created **CharacterController** or navigate to **Window | Animator** in the top menu — it will take us to the **Animator** window where all the magic is happening.

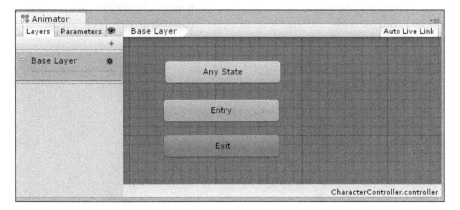

The Mecanim animation system is based around the idea of separating character behavior into different states with assigned animation clips to play while in any particular state. The transitions between states are defined by the set of conditions and are controlled by the **Parameters**.

States

Right click on the empty space of the **Animator** window and navigate to **Create State | Empty**.

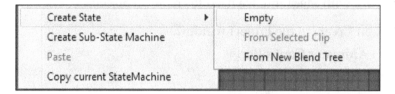

This created our first state, to which we can now assign an animation clip by:

1. Selecting **Create New State**
2. Renaming the state to **Idle** (in the **Inspector**)
3. Assigning the **Idle_Neutral_1** animation clip (**Raw Mocap | Animations | Idle | Idle_Neutral_1**) to the **Motion** parameter in the **Inspector** window

Done, if we just hit **Play**, we will see our character playing the **Idle_Neutral_1** animation in the scene window.

Let's take a step back for a second and see why this is happening.

The first created state is automatically assigned by default and is given an orange color. Try to create a new state by selecting **Run_Impulse** animation clip in the **Project** window and navigating to **Create State | From Selected Clip**. This will create a state; assign it to a selected **Run_Impulse** animation clip and rename it accordingly. Alternatively, we can just drag and drop animation clips from the **Project** to **Animator** window.

We can choose to make the **Run_Impulse** state as the default by right-clicking on it and selecting **Set as Layer Default State**.

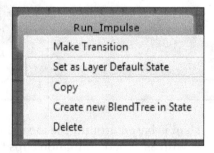

Now we have two animation states, but how do we make a transition from one to the other? The short answer to that is, we have to create one:

1. Right click on the **Idle** state.

2. Select **Make Transition**.

3. Left-click on the **Run_Impulse** state.

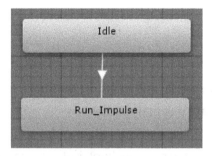

Now these states are connected with a one way transition that will switch from playing the **Idle_Neutral_1** animation to the **Run_Impulse** animation as soon as the transition conditions are met. By default, it's set to make transition as soon as one animation is about to finish playing, also known as **Exit Time**, then it will use the remaining time to blend it with the next animation clip. Give it a try; a character should now play the usual **Idle_Neutral_1** animation and then blend into the **Run_Impulse** animation.

Parameters

The key to controlling animation transitions are custom parameters hidden under a **Parameters** tab at the top left corner of the **Animator** window.

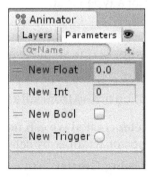

Parameters are used to communicate between the animator and the scripts. Initial parameters can be set in the **Animator** window by pressing a **+** sign and selecting a parameter type to add. Then, programmers can reference this parameter through code and change it. The change in the parameter value will be used to trigger the animation transition by conditions set by the animator. So you see, developers only need to use code to change the value of the parameters, the actual management is controlled by the conditions set in the **Animator** window.

Parameter types

As of Unity V 5.01, we have access to four parameter types, which are as follows:

- **New Int**: These are whole and negative numbers, no fractions
- **New Float**: These are decimal numbers
- **New Bool**: These are the Boolean values of true and false
- **New Trigger**: This is the same as bool, but with an extra benefit of setting itself to false as soon as the transition is completed (we will use the trigger parameter as an example later)

Setting conditions for transitions

So how do we use these parameters to trigger a change in our animation?

Let's start with the most basic example, switching from standing to walking, or, in our case, from the **Idle_Neutral_1** animation to the **Run_Impulse** animation. Our goal is, whenever our character's horizontal velocity is greater than zero, the character should start running; however, he should go back to standing still as soon as the velocity is set back to zero. Here is how we can achieve this:

1. Create a new parameter of a type **Float**.
2. Name it **ZSpeed**.

This parameter will be referenced by script, so make sure that you got the naming correct.

We now need to select the transition arrow from **Idle** to **Run_Impulse** as follows:

1. With the **ZSpeed** parameter created we can now set it under **Conditions** at the bottom of the **Inspector** window by selecting the transition arrow.
2. Set condition to **ZSpeed** being **Greater** than 0.1. This will allow us to have a smooth transition from one animation to another.

3. Uncheck **Has Exit Time** box

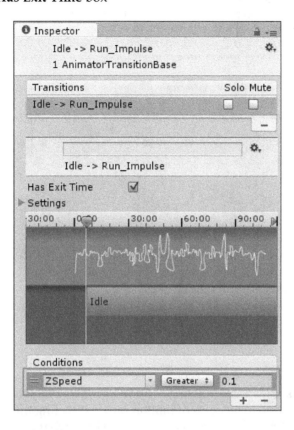

But we aren't done yet, this is just a one way transition and we have yet to revert it to the **Idle** state:

1. Create a transition from the **Run_Impulse** state to **Idle**.

2. Set a condition for this transition for **ZSpeed** to be **Less** than 0.1.

3. Uncheck **Has Exit Time** box

4. Take the script **MoveForward** from the **Chapter 6** folder and assign it as a component of the **Robot GameObject** in the Scene window.

Before we proceed, make sure to check the Loop Time box for the **Run_Impulse** animation by selecting the `Run_Impulse` file (the parent of the animation clip) and going to the Animation tab.

That will do. The **MoveForward** script will take care of the input and changing the **ZSpeed** value; the rest of it will be handled by the transitions that we have just set in the **Animator** window. See it for yourself, hit **Play** and use the *W* key to move forward.

Blend trees

Having animations transition from one to another is all good and dandy; however, in our day and age, due to increase of motion range, blending multiple animations to create new sets of motions is in great demand. That's what blend trees allow us to achieve.

Overview

To better understand animation blending, let's compare it to the animation transition that we've seen in the previous example. With animation transition, we move from one animation to another with a short period of linear interpolation in between; animation blending is that short period of interpolation. Blend trees allow us to set multiple animations and define when and how they are going to affect the character by controlling them with parameters.

The most basic example of the use of the blend trees will be creating a smooth transition from walking to running. If you've ever played a third person game with a gamepad, you might have noticed how smoothly the character goes from walking to running as you slowly tilt the joystick forward — that's the exact feel that we can achieve using blend trees.

Creating a blend tree

Think of the blend trees as a more advanced version of animation states that we've used recently. Their creation process is very similar as well:

1. Right-click on the empty area of the **Animator** window
2. Navigate to **Create State | From New Blend Tree**

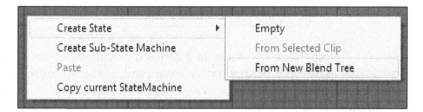

This will create a new block that is deceptively similar to the usual animation state.

Blend tree transitions work in the exact same way as the animation state transition, so much that we can simply convert our previously created **Run_Impulse** state into a **Run** blend tree by:

1. Right clicking on the **Run_Impulse** state.
2. Selecting **Create New Blend Tree in State**.

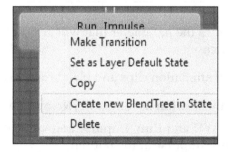

Using the latter method will allow us to preserve all transition conditions we've built before.

You might gain an impression that using the blend trees should be the default way to go. That is however, not true, you only need to rely on them for animation blending, otherwise, stick to using states, they are much simpler.

Inside the blend tree

Double-clicking on the **Blend Tree** will take us inside of it, to where all the blending happens.

As you can see, we already have a slider with a **ZSpeed** parameter control. That is partially because that is the only parameter we have available at the moment. This parameter will be controlling the blend between the animations. Now, with **Blend Tree** selected, let's take a quick look at the **Inspector** view:

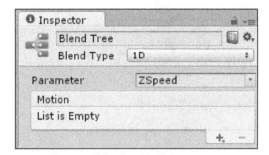

The **Parameter** field specifies the parameter that will be controlling the animation blending (**ZSpeed**, in our case).

Motion contains the list of animation clips and blend trees that we can blend between:

1. Hit the **+** sign of the **Motion** list and add two motion fields.
2. Assign the **WalkFWD** and **Run_Impulse** animation clips to them (**WalkFWD** at the top and **Run_Impulse** at the bottom).

In the **Animator** window, you should now get something like the tree diagram on this figure:

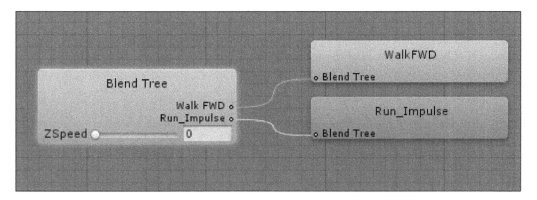

Notice how the **WalkFWD** state is a little bit brighter than the **Run_Impulse** state, with the **ZSpeed** parameter set at 0, and switches as soon as we bring it to a max of 1. That is the sign of blending, with the dominant clip being brighter. Not only that, but even the connecting cord color changes from blue to white based on which animation clip is currently dominant. This is to show how blend trees are going to work; the actual controls to these blends is in the **Inspector** window, that now contains more parameters with previously added clips.

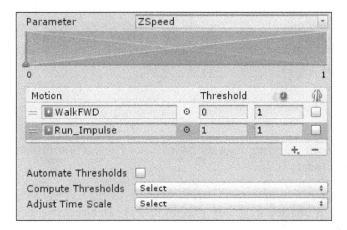

Right below the blending **Parameter**, you will find a pyramid graph that maps added motions to the **Parameter** value. With two animations, we can clearly see that one of them is fully affecting the character at the **ZSpeed** value of 0, while linearly blending into a different animation by the time the parameter value reaches 1.

Left click and hold on any pyramid to see which animation clip it corresponds to.

0 to 1 values are given to parameters by default; we can change that by modifying the maximum **Threshold** value of the motions. All the motions listed, share the animation weight scale, meaning that the threshold is a point at which a single animation gets a 100 percent of the weight while others have no effect at all. This means that there is a value of the animation **Parameter** at which only a single animation will be played. To change the **Threshold** field, make sure to uncheck the **Automate Thresholds** box right below it. Let's change the **Threshold** value of the **Run_Impulse** motion to 4 to better represent what's happening in the scene.

The aforementioned **Automate Thresholds,** is actually a very useful parameter to keep in mind. It's main purpose is to evenly distribute all motions in between their min and max Thresholds. For example, if we were to add an additional motion in between walking and running, set it's **Threshold** to 1 and check **Automate Threshold**, it will instantly jump to 2 (0, 2, 4).

But what is actually happening when you add more than two motions? How do they share the graph? The rules are simple, but they aren't very intuitive from the first glance, it goes like this:

- Each motion must have a **Threshold** at which it becomes the only motion affecting the model

- At any point in time, animations have to share the 100 percent effect on the model

- Each motion down the **Motion** list, should have a higher **Threshold** value than the one above

The first one is very easy to work around; if you don't wish a particular animation to be played without blending, just set its threshold at the point that the animation **Parameter** won't reach.

The second one uses the same principal as, let's say, vertex weight painting; at any point in time, no animation or group of animations can affect the model more than 100 percent; if there are two animations and one of them is affecting the model at 80 percent, the affect of the other animation can't be anything but 20 percent, or there is no blending.

The third is more of a recommendation, if you try to force a lower threshold, it will overlap with over motions and the results will be unpleasant to look at; this also makes sure that you don't have more than two active motions at a time.

But what if there is an actual need to blend more than two motions? Is there a way to do that? Certainly there is, but it might become a little bit hard to manage. The way to do that is by adding another **Blend Tree** to the **Motion** list instead of the **Motion** field.

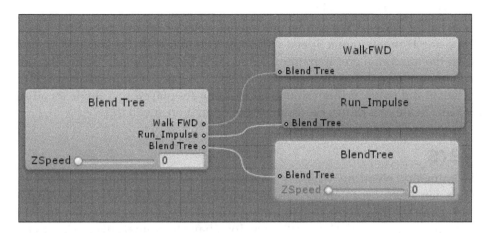

Other blend tree options

There are two other parameters in the motion list that are worth mentioning, next to the threshold:

- A clock sign 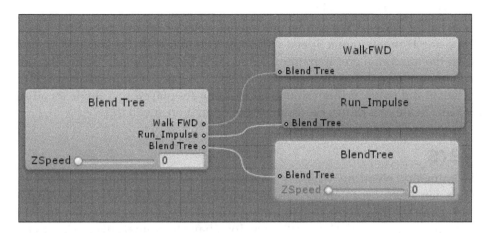 is an animation speed parameter and is particularly useful if you are trying to create a reverse motion, such as creating a landing motion from a jumping motion

- Mirror animation is available only for the humanoid rigs and allows you to mirror animation from one side of the body to another using an avatar

There are also two functions available at the very bottom:

Compute Thresholds is an interesting one. It allows you to automatically compute the threshold values based on the motion at the root of the animation. This basically means that if you have a walking and running animation that moves the character, you can use the **Speed** parameter from the drop-down menu to control them and set up thresholds based on the speed at which the character moves. That is, however, completely useless if there is no root motion. The parameters available are:

1. Speed (the magnitude of velocity)

2. Velocity X

3. Velocity Y

4. Velocity Z

5. Angular Speed (Rad)

6. Angular Speed (Deg)

Adjust Time Scale

If you've added a **Blend Tree** to the motion list, delete it for this parameter to show up. Choosing **Homogeneous Speed** will allow you to rescale the speed of animations based on the minimum and maximum value set in the motion list. Naturally, some animations can have different speed and length; however, blending has to find a compromise and readjust them so that all motions are played in a single blending. **Reset Time Scale** will return the value of the animation speed to 1.

Layers

Unlike animation blending, which is a transition from one animation to another, there is a demand for combining different animations to create new ones. What if we have an attack animation and a running animation, but we don't have the attack while running animation? Thankfully, we don't have to animate every single case scenario, and can choose to combine them instead by using animation layers.

Creation

The **Layer** tab is located at the top right corner of the **Animator** window; it allows us to add and remove layers by hitting the **+** sign or navigating to **Right Click | Delete** as well as modify them.

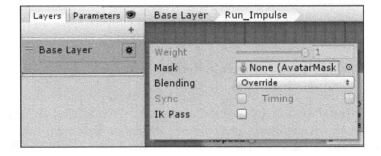

As you can see, there are three parameters to control layers:

- The **Weight** slider controls the effect of each layer on the model.

- **Mask** is the key component of making the combination of layers and animation combining work. By creating an **AvatarMask** with upper body parts enabled, we can make them follow animation instructions given in this particular layer.

- **Blending** is a type of combining that we are planning to use; there are two to choose from:

    ° **Override** will completely ignore any previous layers and overwrite motions with those from this layer for body parts specified in the **Avatar Mask**

    ° **Additive** will add the motion on top of previous layers and their motions

The **Weight** parameter values are important to properly control **Blending**.

Hand waving on move motion

To combine the hand waving and walking animations, we need to create an **AvatarMask** first with only arms and head being affected, as follows:

1. Create a new **AvatarMask** via the **Create** drop-down menu of the **Project** window.
2. Call it **WaveMask**.
3. Under the **Humanoid** property of the **WaveMask** in the **Inspector** window, uncheck everything but left hand, arm, and arm IKs.
4. Return to the **Animator** window and create a new layer called **Wave** under the **Layer** tab.
5. Set **Weight** parameter of the **Wave** layer to 1.

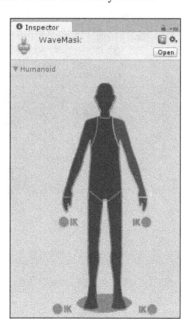

Assign the newly created **WaveMask** to the **Mask** property of the **Wave** layer.

We can now enter the layer by clicking on it and setting up the state for it.

Let's talk a little bit about how we communicate between layers. There is no transition from one layer to another and every layer has to have its own state system that will work independently from other layers. As such, our newly created **Wave** layer will theoretically be in two possible states, the waving state and the passive state, which is all we require of it. Following this logic, we will need to create two states:

- The first state will be called **Passive** and should contain no animation clip and be set to default

- The second state will be called **Waving** and will contain **Robot_Armature | Robot_ArmatureAction Animation Clip** that was imported with our robot

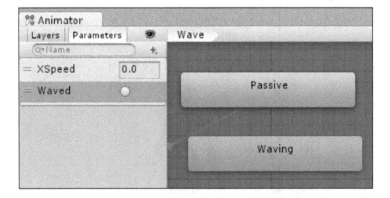

To control the state transition, we will add a new parameter of a trigger type and call it **Waved**. Waved is controlled by code and will be enabled by a click; which transits us to the **Waving** state and uncheck itself immediately (unlike bool, we don't need to bother disabling trigger via code). We also require two transitions from and to the **Passive** state:

- From **Passive** to **Waving** will be controlled by the **Waved** trigger, for that we need to list it under **Conditions**

- From **Waving** to **Passive** should be done as soon as the animation has finished playing, for that, we leave the default **Has Exit Time** under the transition **Conditions**

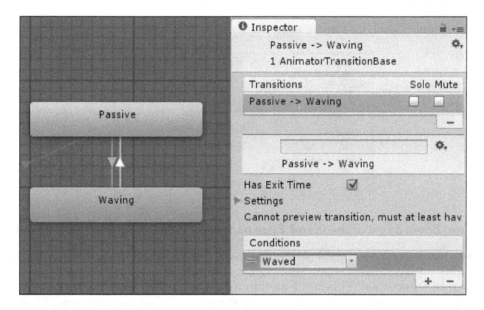

That's about it. With everything set correctly, we should be able to walk/run forward and wave with our hand.

2D blending

Let's get back to blending for just a second, or two. So far, we've looked into a blending mode controlled by a single parameter to make our walk to run transition possible; however, apart from walking in a straight line, we could also benefit from smoothly turning right and left instead of rapidly switching directions. To control this, we require an input from both the vertical and horizontal axes, there are twice as many parameters. Thankfully, Unity has got us covered here by providing 2D blending with various variations to suit our needs.

Blending variations

Looking at the blend tree in the **Inspector** window, you probably have noticed that we've omitted speaking about a parameter called **Blend Type**. This is done on purpose, as most blend types work in a similar fashion, as default **1D** blending that we've looked at, with a layer of their own complexity deriving from working with twice as many parameters. So if, by any chance, you didn't fully grasp how **1D** blending works, I would strongly recommend you go back and look at the examples provided with this chapter, along with the official documentation that comes with Unity (by clicking on the bookmark next to the **BlendTree** name in the **Inspector** window), as the topic we are about to discuss will heavily rely on the previous material.

Feel confident? Good, let's move on!

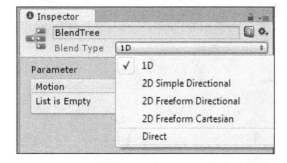

The drop down menu of the **Blend Type** parameter contains four options, as follows:

1D: The blending is controlled by one parameter, the one we've already looked at.

2D Simple Directional: This is the motion that is controlled by two parameters that represent direction. Taking walking as the example, we can use vertical and horizontal speeds as two directional parameters to control the single motion of walking. With this particular 2D blending type, we are limited to a single motion for single direction; therefore, no transition to running is possible.

2D Freeform Directional: This is just like the previous one, but with no single motion restriction. **Walking | Jogging | Running | Sprinting**: You name it and it can be incorporated into this blending type.

2D Freeform Cartesian: This type is better used with controlling parameters that don't represent directions, for something like angles.

Direct: This allows you to directly control the blend parameter. It also allows you to assign a unique parameter to each motion for it to be controlled manually, which is perfect for facial expressions.

It's all about the dots

In the following example, we will use **2D Freeform Directional Blend Type**. We will require a second parameter, which we will call **XSpeed** of a type **Float** and a 3rd motion in a **Motion** list left empty. Your **Inspector** window should now look similar to the one on the following figure:

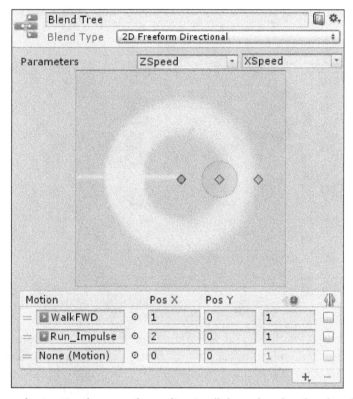

Don't worry about getting the exact color grading, it will change based on the selected element

At first glance, this looks nothing like the simple graph from 1D blending; however, it is actually quite similar to, if not better than, a representation of motion transition.

Take a look at the **Motion** list. Instead of the familiar threshold, we find **Pos X** and **Pos Y**, which are in fact, the thresholds of the first and the second controlled parameters (**ZSpeed** is represented by the X axis and **XSpeed** by the Y axis of the diagram). X and Y motion positions are projected on the 2D plane and represented by the blue icons.

Here is how the mapping works. The origin is located in the center of the diagram with X values increasing from left to right, while Y values do the same from the bottom to the top.

By clicking on any blue icon, you will see a motion that it corresponds to, highlighted in the **Motion** list or vice versa; selecting the motion from the list will highlight it on the diagram.

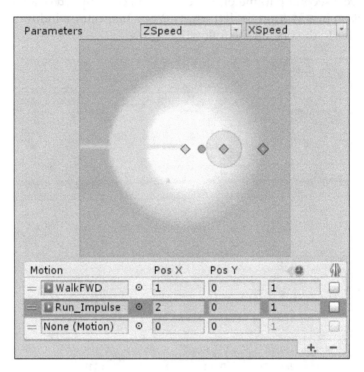

By selecting different motions, you will notice that the color of the diagram changes. The color indicates the weight of the specific motion in certain ranges of X and Y values, with saturation of the blue color indicating the weight influence. With the **Run_Impulse Motion** selected, you can see, on the diagram, that from its threshold position (2,0), it has full control over the animation; however, it gains less influence when closer to the origin, at which the **WalkFWD** motion threshold is set.

The grey icon represents the motion list items that don't have animation clips selected for them (which is the empty clip that we've just created).

The red icon is our current value of two controlled parameters. You can change the values of **ZSpeed** and **XSpeed** on the **Blend Tree** block and see it changing its position accordingly; or you can simply drag it within the diagram yourself and see the character react to the changes in the **Preview** window. You can change the positions of blue and grey icons that way as well.

Last, but not least, there is a circle around the blue icons which is a visual representation of the weight of the particular motion that it is circled around; the bigger the influence, the bigger the radius of the circle. You can try to drag the red icon from one motion to another and see the radius of circles around blue icons change.

Hopefully, this overview will make this diagram a little bit easier to read and manage as we are about to take a look at how to use it to create a full walk/run cycle for our character.

Creating locomotion

Sounds like a little bit too much to take in, well, let's take it in a more digestible form, and take a step–by-step approach to create a working character locomotion:

1. Create a new animation controller and call it **Robot_Locomotion**.
2. Assign it to the **Animator** controller parameter of the robot.
3. Add the **Locomotion** script to the robot components (located in the `Chapter 6` folder) and remove (or deactivate) **MoveForward**.

Setup

Here is a list of motions that we will aim to create:

- Walking (forward and backward)
- Strafing (right and left)
- Turning (while walking and on the spot)

This will allow us to make full use of animations that we have and will require minimum code support.

Regarding parameters, there are three that we will require:

- Float **ZSpeed** and **XSpeed** to control movement and rotation
- Bool **Strafing** to know when our character needs to strafe and to avoid conflict with the walking cycle

Add these parameters to the previously created **Robot_Locomotion** animation controller, the script will take care of the input and will change parameters accordingly, so we don't have to worry about them.

Walking

We will utilize a blend tree to help us create a walking cycle.

Create a new **Blend Tree** and rename it; **Locomotion**.

To control this **Blend Tree**, we will require two parameters, **ZSpeed** and **XSpeed**. One of the parameters is directional (**ZSpeed**), but the other one is controlling the rotation of the character (**XSpeed**) making **2D Freeform Cartesian Blend Type** a logical choice.

As for **Motion** fields, there are 5 that we will require with the following animations clips:

1. Idle_Neutral_1
2. WalkFWD
3. WalkFWD
4. SprintForwardTurnRight_NtrlWide
5. SprintForwardTurnRight_NtrlWide

Having two walking animation clips is not a mistake as it might seem, we will use the same clip twice; for forward and backward motions, by changing the animation speed. To utilize the same animation of turning while moving forward, we will have to mirror one of them by checking the mirror checkbox.

For the parameter values, refer to the following figure:

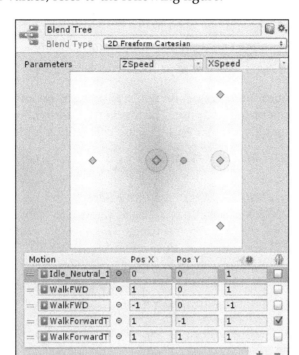

Walking is mapped to the *W*, *A*, *S*, and *D* buttons; try testing it right now.

There are some modifications that need to be applied to the animations in order to avoid some of the issues.

For **Idle_Neutral_1** and **WalkFWD**, check the following boxes:

1. **Loop Time**
2. **Loop Pose**
3. **Bake Into Pose** under **Root Transform Rotation**

The first two are expected; we want our idle animation to loop over and over again. The latter checkbox makes sure that the rotation done by the animation is not affecting the GameObjects transform, to avoid the camera shaking while the character is playing this animation.

For **WalkForwardTurnRight_NtrlWide**:

1. **Loop Time** and **Loop Pose** need to be checked
2. **Cycle Offset** needs to be set to 0.5 for smooth looping
3. **Start** and **End** need to be set to 16 and 362, respectively

Since we are using mocap data there are plenty of motions on animations that we don't need to create proper looping. The **Start** and **End** parameters allow us to isolate that particular region that will give the best results for looping.

Turning

To turn animations, we will take a fraction of the **Idle_NeutralTO45IdleTONeutralIdle** clip and create a new clip from it called **Idle_To_Right** in the **Clips** list of the animation settings. The new clip will start from 280 and end at 315 with **Loop Time** and **Loop Pose** checked.

Two **Idle_To_Right** clips will be added to the **Locomotion** blend tree with the parameters distribution displayed in the following figure. To eliminate small inconsistencies between the **WalkFWD** and **WalkForwardTurnRight_NtrlWide** animations, we are going to speed up the latter to 1.1 (up from 1)

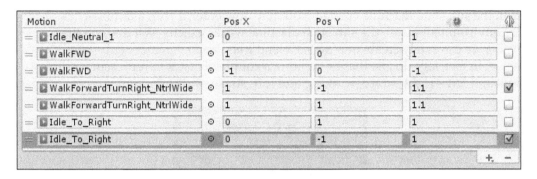

Motion		Pos X	Pos Y	⚓	⚓
= ▶ Idle_Neutral_1	⊙	0	0	1	☐
= ▶ WalkFWD	⊙	1	0	1	☐
= ▶ WalkFWD	⊙	-1	0	-1	☐
= ▶ WalkForwardTurnRight_NtrlWide	⊙	1	-1	1.1	☑
= ▶ WalkForwardTurnRight_NtrlWide	⊙	1	1	1.1	☐
= ▶ Idle_To_Right	⊙	0	1	1	☐
= ▶ Idle_To_Right	⊙	0	-1	1	☑

With this our **Locomotion** blend tree will be complete and we can move to adding strafing.

Strafing

We have two animations for strafing right and left; they will be controlled by **XSpeed** and **Strafing** bool, which will be enabled whenever we press the *Q* or *E* buttons on a keyboard. This might also be a perfect opportunity to introduce the **Sub-State Machine**.

A sub-state machine

Sub-State is essentially a container for other states and a perfect opportunity to group multiple state machines to preserve space and improve readability.

A sub-state machine is created in the same way as the empty state:

1. Right-click on the empty space of the **Animator** window.
2. Select **Create Sub-State Machine** from the drop-down menu
3. Call the sub-state machine **Strafe**

With the sub-state machine created, you may now enter it with a double-click. The environment inside the sub-state machine works exactly as it does on the inside; we can safely create new states, blend trees, and even more sub-states inside. In fact, let's do just that by creating a couple of states to represent strafing right and left—**right_strafe_walking** and **left_strafe_walking**.

Modifying a strafing clip

Just like with the turning animation, we will require a fraction of the existing animation, and then need to create a new clip from it. For that we will use **Strafe_90HipsLeftFaceFwd**:

1. Create a new clip called **Strafe_Right**.
2. Set **Start** and **End** to 90 and 120.
3. Check **Loop Time** and **Loop Pose**.
4. Check **Bake Into Pose** of the **Root Transform Rotation**.
5. Set **Offset** of the **Root Transform Rotation** to -20.8.

The reason for changing the offset is to make this animation more or less loopable. Right now, the animation will move the robot making the start and the end of the animation different; offset will help us to align the start and the end of the clip in a slightly better way.

Transition from and to sub-state

In case you are wondering, the sub-states don't interfere with our ability to translate from one state to another. The **(Up) Base Layer** block that exists in all sub-states will have all transition lines distributed to selected states and vice versa; you may create transitions to any state or blend tree outside of the sub-state by simply creating a transition like we normally did and selecting the one you are trying to connect to, from a drop-down menu.

With that in mind, let's create transitions from and to both **Strafe** states:

1. Create the transition from **Locomotion** to **right_strafe_walking**, that should be controlled by the **Strafing** bool being true, and **ZSpeed** being greater than 0.1.

2. Create a transition from **right_strafe_walking** to **Locomotion** that will be controlled by the **Strafe** bool being **false**.

3. Do the same thing for **left_strafe_walking** with the only difference being, that **ZSpeed** should be less than -0.1.

4. Uncheck **Has Exit Time** on all four transitions

5. Assign the **Strafe_Right** animation clip to both strafing states

6. Make sure that **Mirror** is checked in the **left_strafe_walking** state.

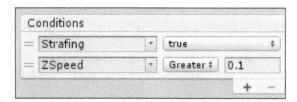

Lastly we are going to add a script to the camera, that will make it follow our character from behind:

1. Find **CameraFollow.js** inside the **Chapter 6** folder

2. Add it to the **MainCamera** GameObject in the **Hierarchy** window

3. Drag and drop the **Robot** GameObject from the scene to the **Char Obj** parameter of the script

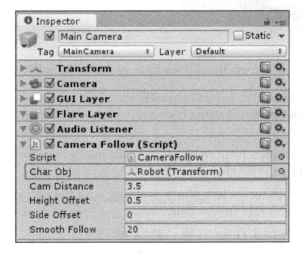

Other parameters can be adjusted to your liking.

That's about it, you now should have an animator controller managing your character while walking, turning, and strafing with minimum scripting support.

Summary

This concludes the introduction to the Mecanim animation system for Unity 5. We've looked into the basic functionality, constructed a motion cycle from scratch and tried out different approaches based on the available animation clips and character rigs. But there is a lot more to be learned if you are really interested in this tool and want to get the best out of it. Programming, despite delegating most of its work to Mecanim, still makes a vital contribution, by setting parameters and supporting more advanced features such as IKs, so make sure to communicate to your programmers constantly if you, yourself, aren't in charge of the code.

In the next chapter, we will continue to look into other features available in Unity that will make our level shine (literally) and relay best practices via tutorials and discussions.

7
Lighting Up the World

If there is one aspect to be named, that has the most effect on the level, it would have to be lighting. It plays a major role in setting the mood, directing players, and allowing us to see things in a pitch-dark environment. Working with lighting isn't as simple as trying to imitate the real-world setup. It's a process that involves a lot of witty tricks and optimization techniques, understanding of how the lighting works in the real world and what's going on under the hood of the rendering engine.

Throughout the chapter, we will look into the following topics:

- Light types, their functionality and application
- Global Illumination
- Light's influence on dynamic and static objects
- Shadows
- Emissive materials
- Baking Lightmaps
- Light probing
- Reflection probes
- Projectors
- Light cookies
- Halos and lenses

Covering every tiny detail might probably take a book of its own, and definitely beyond the scope of an introduction. Instead, we will look at components that make up the lighting system in Unity, discuss the influence of various settings and condition sets on the final result, point out solutions to the most frequent issues and discover interesting techniques to optimize the lighting in the level.

By the end of this chapter, you will be able to use Unity light, bake light into lightmaps, set up shadows, create and set up the light and reflection probes, projector, use flare lenses and light cookies.

Light component

What is a light? The general answer will be that it's an electromagnetic radiation visible to an eye. In Unity, light is a component that changes the brightness of the affected objects allowing them to be seen. You can add a light component to any GameObject by navigating to **Add Component | Rendering | Light**; although, I'll have to say that it is a rare method of doing it. Most of the time, you will be adding the lights to your scene as a separated empty GameObjects by navigating in the top menu to **GameObject | Light**.

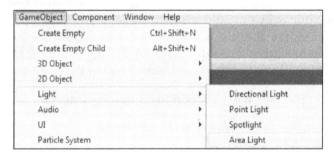

The largest inconvenience of having a light attached to a non-empty GameObject is the fact that its position and rotation are tied to those of the object and you can't control it as flexibly as colliders.

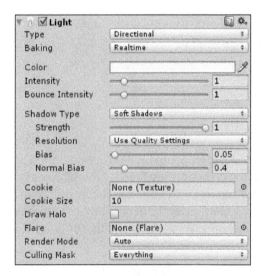

Despite having multiple light types available, most of them have many parameters in common:

- **Type**: This allows you to choose between light types.
- **Color**: This is the color that will be emitted by the light.
- **Intensity**: This controls the brightness of a light.
- **Shadow Type**: This determines the type of shadows that objects, lit by this light, will cast. You have an option of **Hard shadows**, **Soft shadows**, or **No Shadows** at all.

The number of parameters will change based on the type of light you are dealing with.

Light types

Unity has 4 light types that you might already be familiar with and have worked with in different applications. They are **Directional**, **Spot**, **Point** and, **Area** lights. Like artists keeping different types of pencils for different situations, so should you treat light types as just a brush to brighten up the environment and create the mood with.

Point light

Point light is the most basic light type that you might find yourself relying on most of the time. In a way, a Point light is just a shining dot emitting the light within a specified radius. Point light has a vast amount of use. You can use it to simulate realistic lighting, such as candle light, artificially brighten the area, or use it to light up a pickup, or important objects in the level.

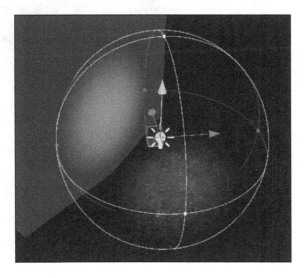

The position of the **Point** light is very important, but rotation, not so much, since the light is emitting from the same spot in all directions.

Point light is controlled by a singular unique parameter, **Range**, which controls the area of effect and emission radius.

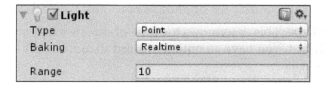

Range is very important to keep in check because the light will not affect any object outside of the sphere radius. In addition to that, light intensity will fade the further it is from the source reaching zero at the sphere's border.

Spot light

This light is represented by a cone with light shining from the top of the cone (light's source) to its base.

This particular light is most commonly used whenever you need a light to shine in a particular direction at a controlled distance — flashlights, projectors, streetlights, and so on.

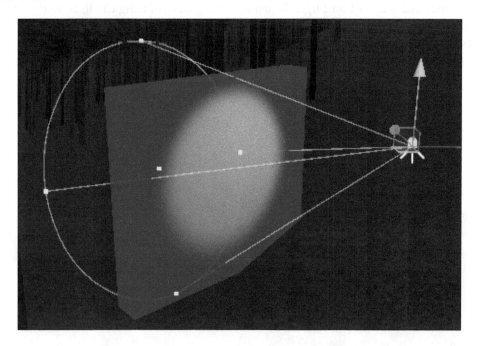

Just like the Point light, the origin of the transform also serves as a light source; however, since Spot light is limited by the cone, it also needs to take full advantage of rotational parameters.

Spot light is controlled by two unique parameters that can be found in the **Inspector** window:

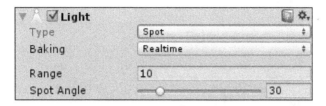

Range controls the height of the cone and how far the light will shine. **Spot Angle** regulates the base radius allowing the light to cover a bigger area.

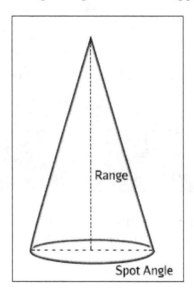

 You should not attempt to use the **Scale** tool to manipulate lights — it will not respond to it. Alternatively, you can manipulate the dots at the bottom of the cone by holding the left mouse button and dragging them to manually adjust the scale.

Spot light brightness isn't constant throughout its range, but fades the further it is from the light source until it reaches zero at the bottom of the cone. As a result, you can sometimes increase the light's brightness by scaling its **Range** instead of **Intensity**. Light will not directly affect the objects outside of the cone.

Directional light

This light shines from infinity to infinity. This basically means its source isn't coming from the light's position, but outside of the scene, far beyond our reach. Because of that, its position in space is completely irrelevant (though you should be able to find it at any time). Its rotation, on the other hand, is crucial to being sure that it shines at the correct angle. It's primarily used to represent sunlight and moonlight.

What's also interesting is that since **Directional** light does not have any beginning or end, its brightness isn't fading in relation to the distance from its position.

Area light

Area Light is emitting light from the entire surface in a facing direction. Should you try to test the Area light right now, you will find that it's not affecting any object. This is because, unlike other light types, it's only available as a baked light without real-time support due to intense processing requirements. All of this comes down to it not being able to affect objects at runtime; yes, a character passing by will not be affected by this light without external help. How to make this light work and a process of baking lights will be discussed later in this chapter. Its uses are limited to emitting light from a surface such as computer screens, TVs, or digital billboards.

As you can notice from the preceding screenshot, **Area Light** is emitting in all directions hitting the wall, floor, and everything within a 180-degree range, but the TV screen on the opposite side.

Area light has a very small number of parameters, but there are two that are unique to it: **Width** and **Height**, which allow control of the size of the rectangle.

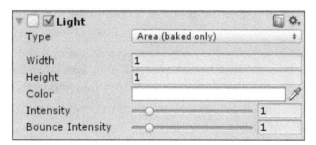

The only way to control the distance at which Area light shines is by changing its **Intensity**, unlike Point or Spot light; you can't control how far it goes.

Ambient light

Apart from lights that can be found in a **Scene** or a **Hierarchy** window, there is one that affects everything, yet isn't easy to locate. The reason why your scene isn't pitch black even with no lights around is because of default ambient light that exists in every scene and can be manipulated by going to **Window | Lighting**.

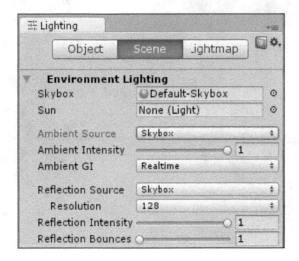

We've visited this window earlier in the book when we were setting the **Skybox** for our level. There are three parameters that affect Ambient light in your scene:

1. **Ambient Source**: This allows you to select one of the three sources of Ambient light:

    ° **Skybox**: This is a default option and it takes the colors of the assigned skybox and uses them for the Ambient light, which creates a realistic looking ambience for the outdoor environments.

    ° **Gradient**: This allows you to manually specify the color for three parameters **Sky Color**, **Equator Color**, and **Ground Color** that will light up the objects from the top, middle, and bottom respectively.

    ° **Color**: This is a simpler version of the previous option with only one color parameter available.

2. **Ambient Intensity**: This controls the strength of the ambient color's influence on the level.

3. **Ambient GI**: This allows you to choose from two options for having Ambient light in either **Realtime** or **Baked**. We will talk about how to work with Global Illumination in future topics.

As you can see, configuring Ambient light is very simple: you either allow Unity to sample colors from the **Skybox** or manually assign colors to it via **Gradient** or **Color** options.

Global Illumination

There are two types of lighting that you will need to take into account if you want to create well lit levels—direct and indirect.

Direct light is the one that is coming directly from the source. Indirect light is created by light bouncing off the affected area at a certain angle with variable intensity. In the real world, the number of bounces is infinite and that is the reason why we can see dark areas that don't have light shining directly at them. In computer software, we don't yet have the infinite computing power at our disposal to be able to use different tricks to simulate the realistic lighting at runtime. The process that simulates indirect lighting, light bouncing, reflections, and color bleeding is known as **Global Illumination (GI)**.

Unity 5 is powered by one of the industry's leading technologies for handling indirect lighting (radiosity) in the gaming industry, called Enlighten by Geomerics. Games such as *Battlefield 3-4*, *Medal of Honor: Warfighter*, *Need for Speed the Run* and *Dragon Age: Inquisition* are excellent examples of what this technology is capable of, and now all of that power is at your fingertips completely for free! Now, it's only appropriate to learn how to tame this new beast.

Preparing the environment

As I've mentioned before, realtime realistic lighting is just not feasible at our level of computing power, which forces us into inventing tricks to simulate it as close as possible, but just like with any trick, there are certain conditions that need to be met in order for it to work properly and keep viewer's eyes from exposing our clever deception. To demonstrate how to work with these limitations, we are going to construct a simple light set up for the small interior scene and talk about solutions to the problems as we go.

For the following example, we will use the **LightmappingInterior** scene that can be found in the **Chapter 7** folder in the **Project** window. It's a very simple interior and should take us no time to set up.

The first step is to place the lights. In this example, we will be required to create two lights: a **Directional** to imitate the moonlight coming from the crack in the dome and a **Point** light for the fire burning in the goblet, on the ceiling.

Tune the light's **Intensity**, **Range** (in **Point** light's case), and **Color** to your liking.

So far so good! We can see the direct lighting coming from the moonlight, but there is no trace of indirect lighting. Why is this happening? Should GI be enabled somehow for it to work? As a matter of fact, it does and here comes the first limitation of Global Illumination—it only works on GameObjects that are marked as **Static**.

Static versus dynamic objects

Unity objects can be of one of the two categories: static or dynamic. Differentiation is very simple: static objects don't move, they stay still where they are at all times, they neither play any animations nor engage in any kind of interactions. The rest of the objects are dynamic.

By default, all objects in Unity are dynamic and can only be converted into static by checking the **Static** checkbox in the **Inspector** window.

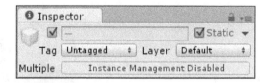

See it for yourself. Try to mark an object as static in Unity and attempt to move it around in the **Play** mode. Does it work?

Global Illumination will only work with static objects; this means, before we go into the "Play" - just like the Play mode right above it. mode, we need to be 100 percent sure that the objects that will cast and receive indirect lights will not stop doing that from their designated positions. However, why is that you may ask, isn't the whole purpose of **Realtime GI** to calculate indirect lighting in runtime? The answer to that would be yes, but only to an extent. The technology behind this is called **Precomputed Realtime GI**, according to Unity developers it precomputes all possible bounces that the light can make and encodes them to be used in realtime; so it essentially tells us that it's going to take a static object, a light and answer a question: "If this light is going to travel around, how is it going to bounce from the affected surface of the static object from every possible angle?"

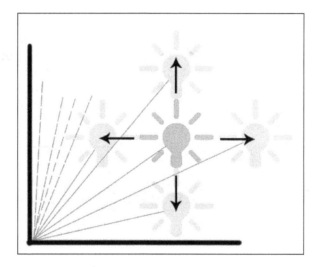

During runtime, lights are using this encoded data as instructions on how the light should bounce instead of calculating it every frame.

 Having static objects can be beneficial in many other ways, such as pathfinding, but that's a story for another time.

To test this theory, let's mark objects in the scene as **Static**, meaning they will not move (and can't be forced to move) by physics, code or even transformation tools (the latter is only true during the **Play** mode). To do that, simply select **Pillar**, **Dome**, **WaterProNighttime**, and **Goblet** GameObjects in the **Hierarchy** window and check the **Static** checkbox at the top-right corner of the **Inspector** window.

Doing that will cause Unity to recalculate the light and encode bouncing information. Once the process has finished (it should take no time at all), you can hit the **Play** button and move the light around. Notice that bounce lighting is changing as well without any performance overhead.

Fixing the light coming from the crack

Before we move on to the next topic, there is one simple issue that could use a quick fix.

The moonlight inside the dome should be coming from the crack on its surface, however, if you rotate the directional light around, you'll notice that it simply ignores concrete walls and freely shines through. Naturally, that is incorrect behavior and we can't have that stay.

We can clearly see through the dome ourselves from the outside as a result of one-sided normals, something we've discussed in the previous chapters during the asset import. Earlier, the solution was to duplicate the faces and invert the normals; however, in this case, we actually don't mind seeing through the walls and only want to fix the lighting issue. To fix this, we need to go to the **Mesh Render** component of the **Dome GameObject** and select the **Two Sided** option from the drop-down menu of the **Cast Shadows** parameter.

This will ignore backface culling and allow us to cast shadows from both sides of the mesh, thus fixing the problem. In order to cast shadows, make sure that your directional light has **Shadow Type** parameter set to either **Hard Shadows** or **Soft Shadows**.

Emission materials

Another way to light up the level is to utilize materials with **Emission** maps. **Pillar_EmissionMaterial** applied to the **Pillar** GameObject already has an **Emission** map assigned to it, all that is left is to crank up the parameter next to it, to a number which will give it a noticeable effect (let's say 3).

Unfortunately, emissive materials are not lights, and precomputed GI will not be able to update indirect light bounce created by the emissive material. As a result, changing material in the **Play** mode will not cause the update.

 Changes done to materials in the **Play** mode will be preserved in the Editor.

Shadows

An important byproduct of lighting is shadows cast by affected objects. No surprises here! Unity allows us to cast shadows by both dynamic and static objects and have different results based on render settings.

By default, all lights in Unity have shadows disabled. In order to enable shadows for a particular light, we need to modify the **Shadow Type** parameter to be either **Hard Shadows** or **Soft Shadows** in the **Inspector** window.

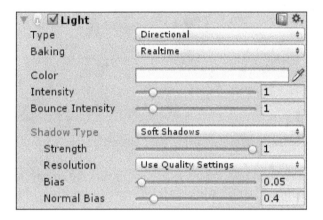

Enabling shadows will grant you access to three parameters:

- **Strength**: This is the darkness of shadows, from 0 to 1.

- **Resolution**: This controls the resolution of the shadows. This parameter can utilize the value set in the **Use Quality Settings** or be selected individually from the drop down menu.

- **Bias** and **Normal Bias** – this is the shadow offset. These parameters are used to prevent an artifact known as **Shadow Acne** (pixelated shadows in lit areas); however, setting them too high can cause another artifact known as **Peter Panning** (disconnected shadow). Default values usually help us to avoid both issues.

Unity is using a technique known as **Shadow Mapping**, which determines the objects that will be lit by assuming the light's perspective—every object that light sees directly, is lit; every object that isn't seen should be in the shadow. After rendering the light's perspective, Unity stores the depth of each surface into a shadow map. In the cases where the shadow map resolution is low, this can cause some pixels to appear shaded when they shouldn't be (Shadow Acne) or not have a shadow where it's supposed to be (Peter Panning), if the offset is too high.

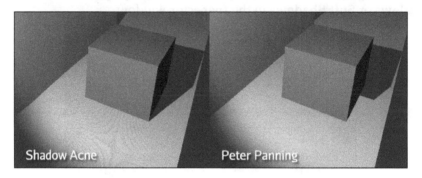

Unity allows you to control the objects that should receive or cast shadows by changing the parameters **Cast Shadows** and **Receive Shadows** in the **Rendering Mesh** component of a GameObject.

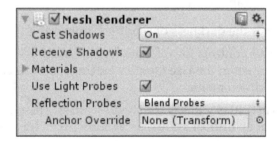

Lightmapping

Every year, more and more games are being released with real-time rendering solutions that allow for more realistic-looking environments at the price of ever-growing computing power of modern PCs and consoles. However, due to the limiting hardware capabilities of mobile platforms, it is still a long time before we are ready to part ways with cheap and affordable techniques such as lightmapping.

Lightmapping is a technology for precomputing brightness of surfaces, also known as baking, and storing it in a separate texture—a lightmap. In order to see lighting in the area, we need to be able to calculate it at least 30 times per second (or more, based on fps requirements). This is not very cheap; however, with lightmapping we can calculate lighting once and then apply it as a texture. This technology is suitable for static objects that artists know will never be moved; in a nutshell, this process involves creating a scene, setting up the lighting rig and clicking **Bake** to get great lighting with minimum performance issues during runtime.

To demonstrate the lightmapping process, we will take the previous scene and try to bake it using lightmapping.

Static versus dynamic lights

We've just talked about a way to guarantee that the GameObjects will not move. But what about lights? Hitting the **Static** checkbox for lights will not achieve much (unless you simply want to completely avoid the possibility of accidentally moving them). The problem at hand is that light, being a component of an object, has a separate set of controls allowing them to be manipulated even if the holder is set to static. For that purpose, each light has a parameter that allows us to specify the role of individual light and its contribution to the baking process, this parameter is called **Baking**.

There are three options available for it:

- **Realtime**: This option will exclude this particular light from the baking process. It is totally fine to use real-time lighting, precomputed GI will make sure that modern computers and consoles are able to handle them quite smoothly. However, they might cause an issue if you are developing for the mobile platforms which will require every bit of optimization to be able to run with a stable frame rate. There are ways to fake real-time lighting with much cheaper options, which we will discuss later. The only thing you should consider is that the number of realtime lights should be kept at a minimum if you are going for maximum optimization. Realtime will allow lights to affect static and dynamic objects.

- **Baked**: This option will include this light into the baking process. However, there is a catch: only static objects will receive light from it. This is self-explanatory — if we want dynamic objects to receive lighting, we need to calculate it every time the position of an object changes, which is what **Realtime** lighting does. **Baked** lights are cheap, calculated once we have stored all lighting information on a hard drive and using it from there, no further recalculation is required during runtime. It is mostly used on small situational lights that won't have a significant effect on dynamic objects.

- **Mixed**: This one is a combination of the previous two options. It bakes the lights into the static objects and affects the dynamic objects as they pass by. Think of the street lights: you want the passing cars to be affected; however, you have no need to calculate the lighting for the static environment in realtime. Naturally, we can't have dynamic objects move around the level unlit, no matter how much we'd like to save on computing power. Mixed will allow us to have the benefit of the baked lighting on the static objects as well as affect the dynamic objects at runtime.

The first step that we are going to take is changing the **Baking** parameter of our lights from **Realtime** to **Baked** and enabling **Soft Shadows**:

You shouldn't notice any significant difference, except for the extra shadows appearing.

The final result isn't too different from the real-time lighting. Its performance is much better, but lacks the support of dynamic objects.

Dynamic shadows versus static shadows

One of the things that get people confused when starting to work with shadows in Unity is how they are being cast by static and dynamic objects with different **Baking** settings on the light source. This is one of those things that you simply need to memorize and keep in mind when planning the lighting in the scene. We are going to explore how different **Baking** options affect the shadow casting between different combinations of static and dynamic objects:

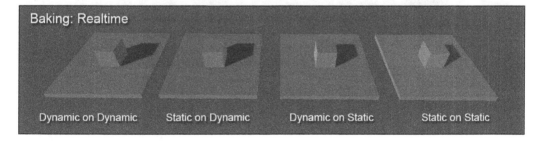

As you can see, real-time lighting handles everything pretty well; all the objects are casting shadows onto each other and everything works as intended. There is even color bleeding happening between two static objects on the right.

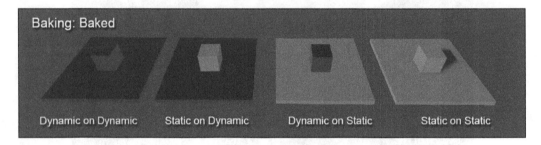

With **Baked** lighting the result isn't that inspiring. Let's break it down.

Dynamic objects are not lit, and we've talked about that previously. If the object is subject to change at runtime, we can't preemptively bake it into the lightmap; therefore, lights that are set to **Baked** will simply ignore them.

Shadows are only cast by static objects onto static objects. This correlates to the previous statement that if we aren't sure that the object is going to change we can't safely bake its shadows into the shadow map.

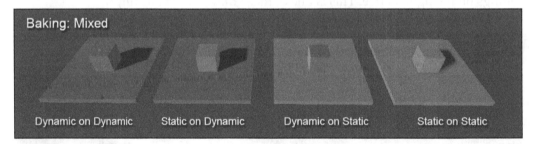

With **Mixed** we get a similar result as with real-time lighting, except for one instance: dynamic objects are not casting shadows onto static objects, but the reverse does work: static objects are casting shadows onto the dynamic objects just fine, so what's the catch? Each object gets individual treatment from the Mixed light: those that are static are treated as if they are lit by the Baked light and dynamic are lit in realtime. In other words, when we are casting a shadow onto a dynamic object, it is calculated in realtime, while when we are casting shadow onto the static object, it is baked and we can't bake a shadow that is cast by the object that is subject to change. This was never the case with real-time lighting, since we were calculating the shadows at realtime, regardless of what they were cast by or cast onto. And again, this is just one scenario that you need to memorize.

Lighting options

The **Lighting** window has three tabs: **Object**, **Scene**, and **Lightmap**. For now we will focus on the first one.

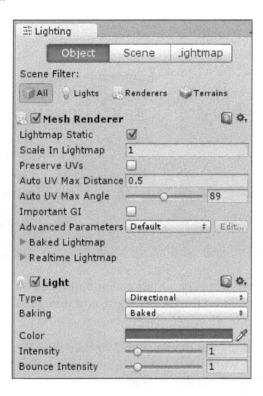

The main content of an **Object** tab is information on objects that are currently selected. This allows us to get quick access to a list of controls, to better tweak selected objects for lightmapping and GI.

You can switch between object types with the help of **Scene Filter** at the top; this is a shortcut to filtering objects in the **Hierarchy** window (this will not filter the selected GameObjects, but everything in the Hierarchy window).

As was mentioned earlier, all GameObjects need to be set to **Static** in order to be affected by the lightmapping process; this is why the **Lightmap Static** checkbox is the first in the list for **Mesh Renderers**. If you haven't set the object to static in the **Inspector** window, checking the **Lightmap Static** box will do just that.

The **Scale in Lightmap** parameter controls the lightmap resolution. The greater the value, the bigger the resolution given to the object's lightmap, resulting in better lighting effects and shadows. Setting the parameter to 0 will result in an object not being affected by lightmapping. Unless you are trying to fix lighting artifacts on the object, or going for the maximum optimization, you shouldn't touch this parameter; there is a better way to adjust the lightmap resolution for all objects in the scene; **Scale in Lightmap** scales in relation to global value.

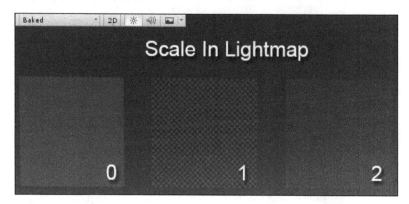

The rest of the parameters are very situational and quite advanced, they deal with UVs, extend the effect of GI on the GameObject, and give detailed information on the lightmap.

For lights, we have a baking parameter with 3 options: **Realtime**, **Baked**, or **Mixed**. Naturally, if you want this light for lightmapping, **Realtime** is not an option, so you should pick **Baked** or **Mixed**.

Color and **Intensity** are referenced from the **Inspector** window and can be adjusted in either place.

Baked Shadows allows us to choose the shadow type that will be baked (**Hard**, **Soft**, **Off**).

Bringing lights into the level

Now that you've been introduced to the lights, it's about time to start adding them to your level. The general rule when lighting the level is to start with dominant lights (usually directional sunlight/moonlight) and continue in descending order. Don't try to tweak multiple lights at the same time, focus on one and then on another once you are satisfied. The more lights you add, the more color mixing will happen and you might find yourself in a situation of not being able to figure out what to tweak to get the desired effect.

If you wish to challenge yourself, try to bake some of the areas that your character will not be moving into and optimize lighting to the best of your ability.

Light probes

Realtime Global Illumination works great with static objects, but what about dynamic? Precomputed GI will not be able to calculate the bounces if the object's location is subject to change; thankfully, there is another way out with a use of **Light Probes**.

Light probes are spheres that are sampling the light in the area and transfer it to the dynamic objects nearby.

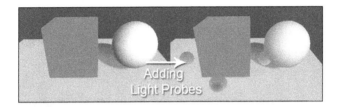

To create light probes, go to **GameObject | Light Probe Group**.

This will create four interconnected light probes positioned in the form of a cube.

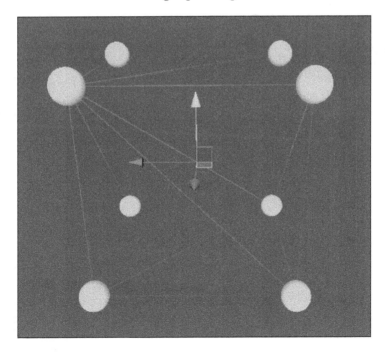

Probes are controlled in the exact way as other GameObjects in the scene:

- Click to select (*Shift* and click to add a new one to selection)
- *Ctrl* + *D* to duplicate
- The *Delete* key to delete

For the GameObject to be affected by light probes, it needs to be dynamic and have **Use Light Probes** checked in the **Mesh Renderer** component.

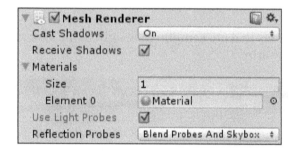

There isn't much to add about the light probes, they are extremely easy to use and have a straightforward application. It's important to position them in the places where you expect the dynamic objects to pass by to transfer lighting on to them.

Reflection probes

Reflections are very important to create believable environments where objects feel connected to each other. Reflection probes work in a similar way as light probes in a sense that they sample the surrounding environment and send this information to the affected objects to reflect.

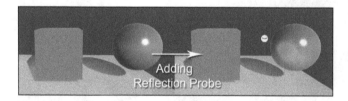

Unlike light probes, reflection probes are useful for both static and dynamic objects.

Whenever you place a reflection probe in the scene, it samples the environment around itself and creates a cubemap that is later used by the objects that are using it. In order to find out information about which reflection probe is affecting any particular GameObject, we need to look at the **Mesh Renderer** component once again.

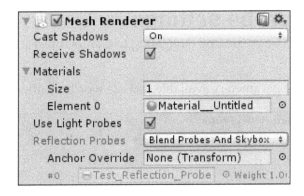

The **Reflection Probes** parameter determines how this GameObject will work with reflection probes, there are four options available:

Off: Choosing this option will cause reflection probes to stop affecting this object.

Simple: GameObject can only be affected by a single reflection probe.

Blend Probes: This allows the object to be affected by multiple reflection probes.

Blend Probes and Skybox: This works just like the previous one but also includes the skybox in the blending.

Every reflection probe has a bounding box, everything that is within this box will be included in the sampling and will have a probe assigned to it (you can see the list of assigned probes at the bottom of the **Mesh Renderer** component). Sometimes reflection probe boxes can overlap; in this case, the objects located at the overlapping area that have either **Blend Probes** or **Blend Probes and Skybox** selected for the **Reflection Probes** parameter will receive reflection from multiple reflection probes. The Reflection probe that covers the greater area of an object will have greater blending weight (this concept is similar to the animation blending we've talked about in the previous chapter).

If you want objects that are outside of the bounding box to be affected by the reflection probe, simply assign a **Transform** component reference to the **Anchor Override** parameter. This will take the information about the reflection probes affecting the referenced object and assign the same values to the object outside of the bounding box (this also includes the blending information).

Reflection probe settings

Reflection probes can be created by navigating to **GameObject | Light | Reflection Probe** in the top menu.

There are quite a few parameters available that are worth mentioning.

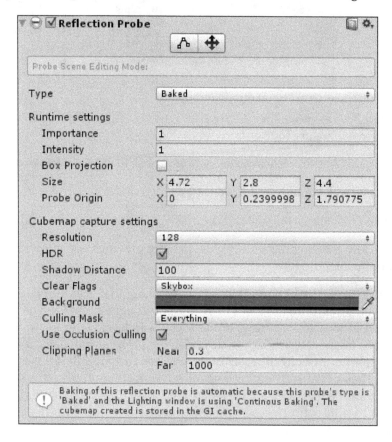

Types of reflection probes

Just as with lights and shadows, we can choose to update reflection probes at realtime, bake them or control them via code by assigning custom cubemaps. The **Type** parameter allows us to choose between three options: **Realtime**, **Baked**, and **Custom**.

Unlike lights, there is a much greater difference in performance between **Realtime** and **Baked** reflection probes. Choosing the **Realtime** option will expose **Refresh Mode** and **Time Slicing** parameters that will allow us to have a better control, by specifying how often the update should happen and how cube map should be updated; however, let's focus on the difference between the two and why you need to choose.

Take a look at the following screenshot:

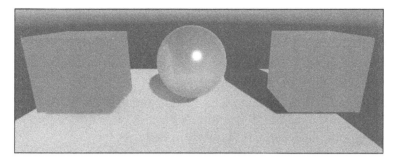

You can clearly see that the sphere in the middle is properly reflecting the cube on the left; however, it ignores the one on the right. Why is this happening? The cube on the left, the one that's being reflected is a static object. The cube on the right is a dynamic object. With our **Baked** type reflection probe, we can't update the reflection at runtime; therefore, dynamic objects that can go in and out of the reflection range are ignored by the reflection probe when it samples the environment. In order to have both cubes properly reflected, we need to change **Type** to **Realtime** and set the exposed **Reflection Mode** parameter to **Every Frame**.

Runtime settings

These settings are affecting the objects that are using the cubemap of this particular probe:

- **Importance**: This parameter helps **Mesh Renderer** to choose which reflection probe to use whenever it has an option. Let's say we have reflection probe A with a gigantic bounding box and a reflection probe B with a smaller area located within the bounds of the previous one. If the **Importance** parameters of both reflection probes are equal, they will be blended based on the percent of the affected area; however, if probe B has a higher **Importance** value, it will completely overwrite the effect of the probe A.

- **Intensity**: This parameter controls how powerful the reflection is.

- **Box Projection**: By default, reflection is treated as if it's coming from far away. **Box Projection**, mostly utilized in enclosed places, allows the addition of proper depth to the reflection.

Size and **Probe Origin** control the bounding box of the probe. **Probe Origin** is in relation to the probe's transform (works similar to the **Center** parameter of the **Box Collider** component).

Cubemap capture settings

There are a few parameters worth mentioning:

- **Resolution**: This sets the resolution for the cubemap
- **Shadow Distance**: This is a distance in Unity units at which the reflection probe will pick up shadows
- **Culling Mask**: This allows you to include and exclude objects from being included in the cubemap reflection by putting them on separate layers and checking/unchecking them in the **Culling Mask** list

Positioning of a reflection probe

One of the greatest limitations of the reflection probes is that they apply the reflection on to the objects not from the location of each individual object, but from the reflection samples of each probe's location.

If you are desperate for realistic reflections, you can opt to add reflection probes as components to each individual object by navigating to **Add Component | Rendering | Reflection Probe**. Just make sure that the bounding boxes of the probes don't include other probes.

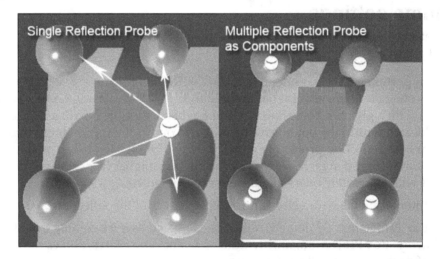

Needless to say that adding a reflection probe as a component to every GameObject in the level might cause performance issues; therefore, it is recommended that you make the best use of reflection probes by covering an area as big as possible and adding new ones in places where the difference will be noticeable (such as caves or next to important objects that stand out visually).

Continuous baking

In Unity 5, the lighting is being processed automatically in the background after you've changed anything in the scene that could affect the final result. It's a very neat and interesting feature that works surprisingly fast on modern computers. However, despite its fantastic optimization, it is still noticeable, especially when you are working with reflections that take much longer time to be calculated compared to lights. To enable calculation on demand, do the following:

1. Open the **Lighting** window (**Window | Lighting**).
2. At the bottom of the **Scene** tab, uncheck the **Continuous Baking** option.

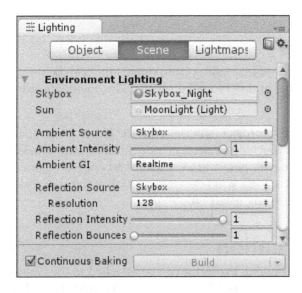

Now, if you need to calculate the lighting, you can click on the **Build** button next to it and execute the process on demand.

When you disable the **Continuous Baking** feature and rely on **build on demand** with the **Build** button, Unity will be taking a snapshot of the level's lightmap, create a folder that has the same name as the level and store the snapshot there.

Adding probes to the level

Now that we've briefly covered the light and reflection probes, it's about time to include them in our level. Look at different places that the character can visit and add the net of light probes there, to sample the light around that area.

Do the same thing with reflection probes, try to cover as big an area as possible with them and add new ones in places where the reflection will noticeably change.

It order to keep track of all probes, I recommend creating a new layer called **Probes** and assigning all probes to it. This way you can hide them in the editor when you are done placing them.

Projectors

Unity has no shortage of interesting components that can be used in creative ways to produce interesting and very useful results. The one in question here is called the projector.

The projector is used to project material onto the object to create interesting effects such as decals, cinema screen projection, or even shadows. The latter is well known for being hyped by developers and very useful whenever you're in need of a cheap dynamic shadow effect. We will take a closer look at the component itself and showcase some interesting uses of it.

Basic application

Being a normal component, **Projector** can be attached to the GameObject by going to: **Add Component** | **Effects** | **Projector** in the **Inspector** window or **Component** | **Effects** | **Projector** from the top menu.

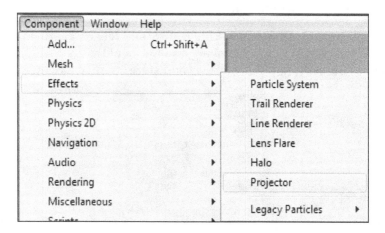

Create an empty GameObject and add the **Projector** component to it.

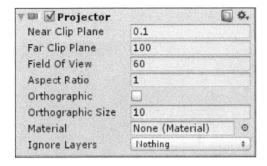

Using the projector becomes very intuitive if you treat it as a real projector that can project an image from a source to a surface. However, there are few noticeable distinctions; the most noticeable being the way it influences the objects that come within contact.

The **Scale** tool has no effect on the projector, so the only way to control its area of effect is via the component parameters:

Near Clip Plane and **Far Clip Plane** controls the distance from the object from which the cone will start and end, allowing you to set how far the projection will go and where it can start from.

Field Of View controls the width of the cone, while **Aspect Ratio** allows you to set its relation to height (a value of 2 will make height twice the width).

Checking the **Orthographic** checkbox will turn the cone into a cube and enable the use of **Orthographic Size** parameters that controls the cube's size.

There are quite a few parameters, but the latter two are the ones that really matter:

Material sets the material that will be projected. Make sure to count in the **Material** properties when considering projecting something, naturally, different **Materials** will have different results.

Ignore Layers allows you to select layers that will be affected by this projector; if you don't specify the exact layers, it will project the texture on everything that is within the affected area and that might bring some unexpected results.

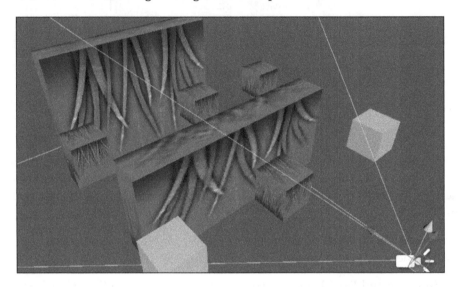

As you can see, from the preceding screenshot, the projector isn't casting the material from the source to the destination through objects on the way, but rather applies specified material on all objects within the affected area.

Other applications

As was mentioned earlier, the projector can go a long way if used creatively. To get the most out of it, we will require some additional assets available in **Standard Assets**:

1. Go to **Assets | Import Assets | Effects**.
2. Hit **Import** to get the required assets to **Standard Assets | Effects | Projectors**.

With the new package, we get access to two new shaders that are specifically made to be used with the **Projector** component—**Projector Light** and **Projector Multiply**.

Projector Light can be used to create efficient light effects and in some occasions, be used instead of **Spot Light**. Use the **Blob Light Projector** prefab and see it for yourself.

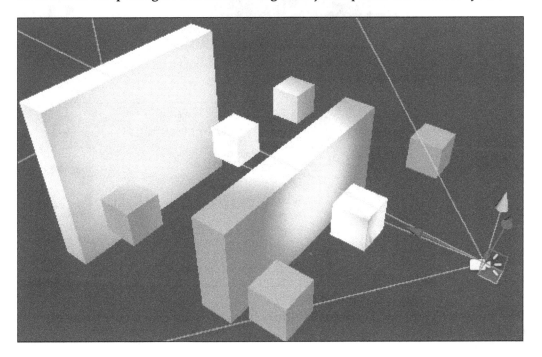

Projector Multiply on the other hand is perfectly suited to create artificial shadows. One in particular is the shadow underneath the character that would have otherwise required a dynamic lighting to create. Use **Blob Shadow Projector** and add the character object layer to the **Ignore** list of the **Projector** component to achieve this effect.

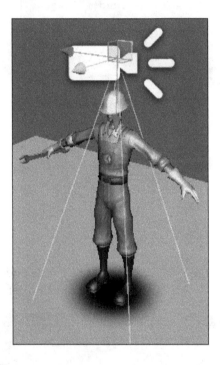

The key to using new shaders are textures.

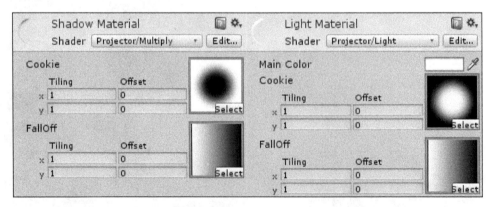

Both **Projector/Light** and **Projector/Multiply** have two required texture parameters—**Cookie** and **FallOff**.

Cookie is a texture that will be projected onto the surface. Make sure to set the created texture **Wrap Mode** to **Clamp** in order to get it to work right (you can always refer to how **Light** and **Shadow** textures are set, if in doubt). **FallOff** is an optional texture that lets you specify the falloff gradient. **Projector/Light** has a **Main Color** parameter that allows us to set the color of the light we are trying to fake.

Lighting effects

Unity lights support various lighting effects, namely halos, cookies, and flares to simulate various tones or light types. Some of the standard packages contain additional materials that can be used to assist us in the upcoming examples.

We will use assets inside the **Effects** folder to demonstrate the abilities of light cookies and flares.

Light cookies

Default lighting doesn't have any texture; it simply emits the photons in specified directions with specified color. Getting a vivid effect of light shining through the mosaic surface can be achieved with light cookies.

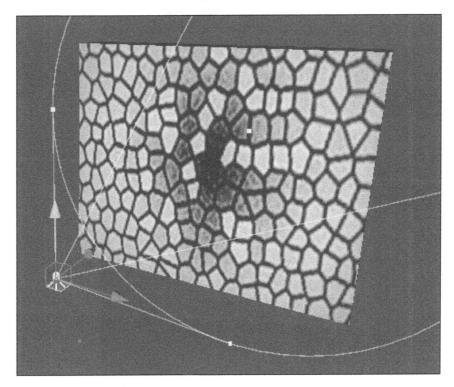

Light cookies, just like projectors, are amazing at creating cheap light effects, these grayscale textures will control your lighting and assist skillful artists at enhancing the level.

Assets from imported standard packages contain few very useful textures that can be applied to the light in order to create different effects:

Light Cookie is just a grayscale texture with all the options to control it assigned to the creation process and import settings. In the light options, you simply need to assign the texture to the **Cookie** parameter in order for it to work.

The **Cookie** parameter will not show up if you have the **Baking** parameter set to **Baked**.

Despite its simplicity, there are few things that you need to keep in mind in order to get light cookies to work properly. To talk about that process, we will create a light cookie texture.

Creating light cookies

The first thing to remember is that all cookie textures need to be perfect squares. You will not be able to even assign a texture to the parameter if one side is bigger than the other.

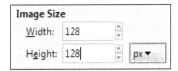

On the other hand, the size of the texture is completely up to you, although a power of 2 is strongly recommended.

As mentioned earlier, the texture itself is a grayscale with brighter color indicating the intensity of the light in that area. For this example, I will go with something impressionistic (or at least, I hope so):

One thing that you should watch out for is texture bleeding. That is a common problem for **Cookie** textures that can be solved by leaving a black border around the edges of the image. If you see texture bleed, simply make that border thicker, which should solve the problem most of the time.

No alpha channel is required; we will simply ask Unity to generate one from grayscale.

On texture import, there are few options that we need to pay extra attention to:

Texture Type should be set to **Cookie**, needless to say, it's specifically created for that type of texture.

With the **Cookie** texture type, we now get access to the **Light Type** parameter, where we can make our texture adjust to a specific light type we are planning to use it on (otherwise we will not be able to use cookies with a Spot light).

Lastly, we need to check the **Alpha from Grayscale** box to make sure that our alpha is set properly.

Now we can assign our texture to a **Cookie** parameter of the **Light** component and enjoy the effect.

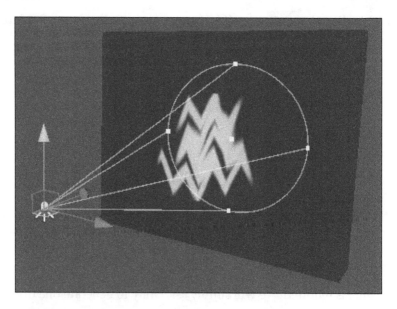

That is it! No bleeding or other weird artifacts. Setting **Texture Type** to **Cookie** automatically sets it to **Clamp** mode. Try to experiment with our own textures and take a look at those available in the imported standard package.

One might wonder at this point as to whether they can achieve the same result with the projector and how they decide which one to use.

The short answer is that you can achieve a similar effect to a certain degree with a projector using the same texture. Although, the import setting will have to be changed by changing **Texture Type** to **Texture** or **Advanced** and using **Projector/ Light** material; the proof of this is shown in the following screenshot:

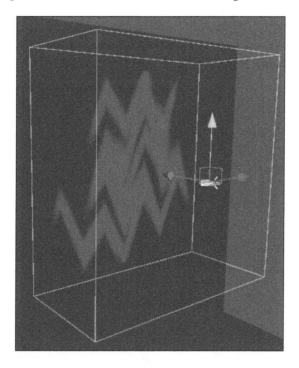

However, there are some obvious limitations that you will not be able to workaround:

1. **Spot** and **Point** lights cannot be simulated this way.
2. **Projector** is not actually a light, it's just projecting a material; therefore, it has limited control over brightness and intensity.

If you can live with these limitations and are simply in need of cheap dynamic (fake) light, then feel free to use a projector over a light cookie, otherwise, don't bother.

Flares and halos

There are a couple of interesting effects that you can assign to lights.

Halo

The most simplistic is a **Halo**.

To enable it, simply check the corresponding checkbox in the **Inspector** window.

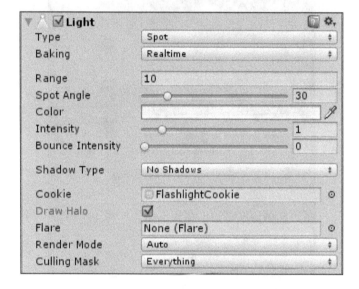

This will draw a spherical light zone around the light source.

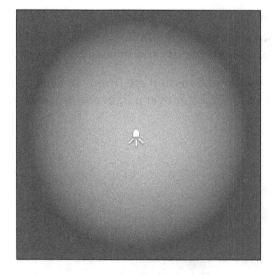

This zone can be controlled by the same parameters that control the light: radius, color and brightness are tied to **Range**, **Color**, and **Intensity**, respectively.

Halo is also not a light, just an effect; therefore, it can't replace a Point light.

The good news is that the Halo effect can be attached to other objects without light, but via the **Halo** component (**Add Component | Effects | Halo**).

The **Halo** component options are fewer, but they serve a similar purpose and achieve similar results as the **Light** component's counterparts.

Flare

This one is a lot more complicated to create; therefore, we will focus on those provided within the standard package. The available flares have pretty amazing effects that can be used in various situations; here is how it enhances our level by applying **50mmZoom** flare to a directional light representing the sun.

Flare itself is a special asset of a type **Lens Flare** and it can be created via the **Create** menu of the **Project** window or by going to **Assets | Create | Lens Flare**.

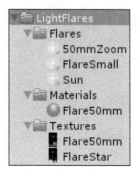

In order to operate a flare, it requires a texture with image effects sliced in one of the six supported layouts (refer to the official documentation for more information about layouts). Here is a simple flare asset **Small Flare**.

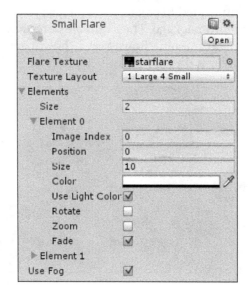

The final result of the flare is a composition of elements specified in the **Elements** array. The images for each element are specified by the **Image Index** parameters. Image indexes are bound to the selected texture layout, with each layout storing pixel coordinates for each index. This is why you need to consider the texture layout whenever you are creating the texture for a flare and arrange images accordingly.

The following is an example of **1 Large 4 Small layout** used for **Small Flare**:

```
┌───────────────┐
│               │
│       0       │
│               │
├───────┬───────┤
│       │       │
│   1   │   2   │
│       │       │
├───────┼───────┤
│       │       │
│   3   │   4   │
│       │       │
└───────┴───────┘
```

Each individual component can then be individually adjusted by element parameters. And that is how flares work in a nutshell.

Just as with Halos, you can attach flares to any object with the **Lens Flare** component (**Add Component | Effects | Lens Flare**).

However, there is one problem with that—flares are blocked by colliders, so make sure you disable the collider on the object that has a lens component attached to it.

Another interesting effect is the one that flares have on directional light—flares will appear based on the camera position (in the case of the Sun, you need to look at the sun, with a **Main Camera**, for a flare to appear). The **Lens Flare** component can imitate that effect by checking the **Directional** checkbox.

Summary

Lighting is a difficult process that is deceptively easy to learn, but hard to master. In Unity, lighting isn't without its issues. Attempting to apply real-world logic to 3D rendering will result in a direct confrontation with limitations posed by imperfect simulation. In order to solve issues that may arise, one must first understand what might be causing them, in order to isolate the problem and attempt to find a solution. We attempted to achieve this in this chapter by looking at different light types, discussing what causes lighting to work in a certain manner, and what behavior should be expected from various settings. Knowing these nuances will help you to better apply the available tools and technologies necessary to achieve the desired results with your lighting rigs; and knowledge of projectors, light cookies, halos, and flares will allow enhancing the result even further.

Alas, there are still a lot of topics left uncovered that are outside of the realm of an introduction. If you wish to learn more about lighting, I would point you again to the official documentation and developer blogs, where you'll find a lot of useful information, tons of theory, practical recommendations, as well as in-depth look into all light elements discussed in this chapter.

In the next chapter, we will talk about another important component of level ambience — sound.

8
Bringing the Sound

The sound effects aren't something you immediately think about when starting a level; they are usually decided closer to the end of the planning, or, in some scenarios, when the level is already in production, which is often the reason why they're being neglected. That is a huge shame, since well-tuned and arranged sound effects can greatly benefit the level in creating substance and reinforcing the theme.

With Unity 5, we have great tools that can help us in achieving a varied and rich sound design for our levels. Throughout this chapter, we will look into different topics associated with sound design in Unity and will learn the following:

- How does sound work in Unity 5
- Creating and configuring sound receivers and emitters
- Starting with the audio mixer to arrange, mix, and manipulate sound effects
- How to utilize reverb zone and audio filters to add environmental influence

Sound effects may be an alien topic to many developers; therefore, we will only cover the material that doesn't require knowledge of audio design and examples that you can recreate and test without reliance on code. However, the topics you will learn in this chapter will help you start with, and guide you into, the areas you might want to explore in pursuit of more complicated sound setups; and if you are already familiar with the topic, you may find a way to apply that knowledge inside of Unity.

Audio sources and receivers

The way the audio works in Unity is no different from the real life that it's trying to imitate, and it all comes down to collaboration between objects that emit sounds and those that receive them. In Unity, both of them are components, known as **Audio Source** and **Audio Listener**. Being components, they can be attached to any GameObject via the **Add Component** menu in the **Inspector** window:

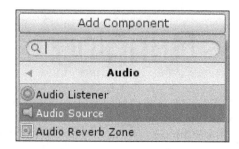

Alternatively, you can create an empty GameObject with an audio source or reverb zone by navigating to **GameObject** | **Audio** in the top menu.

 For future references, we will use the **Audio Source** created from the top menu.

Audio listener

Unlike the audio source, we already have an **Audio Listener** present in every scene by default; it's attached to the **MainCamera** object.

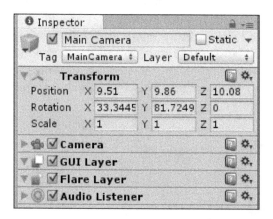

Audio Listener doesn't have any parameters and all it needs to function is to simply exist in the scene. There is, however, one rule that should be followed when dealing with audio listeners:

 The Scene always has to have exactly one active audio listener.

If you've accidentally placed two, Unity will send you a message and will ignore the other one upon play. The reasoning behind that is quite simple—you can't play the same sound to multiple listeners and expect them to be perceived correctly; it simply won't sound right and you will not be able to orientate yourself in the space.

There are some niche situations that you will have to work around using clever coding—imagine looking at the monitor screen of a security camera. In this situation, we need to hear actions happening around us, as well as in the area that we see with the camera. This can be cheated by adjusting the audio sources from the camera area to sound like they are close by or forcibly move them to be played from the speaker location. We aren't going to imitate that specifically, but most similar scenarios can be cheated in one way or another to work around this limitation.

Audio source

The listener picks up every sound that reaches its location. In order to emit that sound, we need to have an **Audio Source** that will control how this sound will be emitted in order to make sure that the **Listener** picks it up.

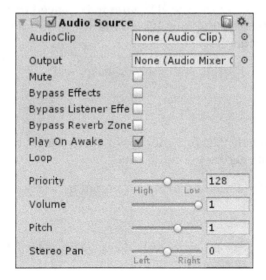

Let's walk-through some of its properties and how they influence the sound:

- **AudioClip**: This is an audio file that will be played by **Audio Source** (we will look into it shortly).

- **Output**: This allows us to control this sound effect with **Audio Mixer** by assigning an **Audio Group** to this parameter (again, we will talk more about this when we look at **Audio Mixer**).

- **Mute**: This simply mutes the sound effect.

- **Bypass Effects**, **Bypass Listener Effects** and **Bypass Reverb Zone**: This allows us to bypass (ignore) all effects and filters applied to **Audio Source**.

- **Play On Awake**: Checking this box will play the sound upon starting the game. That is also the only way, outside of scripting, to force the sound to play.

- **Loop**: This loops the audio track, good for ambient music.

- **Priority**: This one is important. Despite having no limitations to a number of sound emitters, we need to keep in mind that some of them may overlap, and a system will have to make a decision which one to give a priority to when playing. This parameter will allow you to control this decision making by giving the sounds that you never want to be interrupted a lower value (such as background music). The priority ranges from 0 to 256, but it's much easier to use a slider with indicators to intuitively set the correct value.

- **Volume**: This sets the overall volume of this sound.

- **Pitch**: This controls the play speed. It ranges from -3 to 3 with 1 being the default.

- **Stereo Pan**: This controls the 2D sound to be played from the right or left side of a stereo set up (for 3D sounds, it will be adjusted based on the listener position).

These parameters are the barebones of the audio source.

Audio clips

Every supported audio file that you import, will immediately become an **Audio Clip**, which is simply a container for the audio data.

There are four audio file formats that are supported by Unity: `.aiff`, `.ogg`, `.wav`, and `.mp3`.

 Unity also supports tracker modules of the following formats: `.xm`, `.mod`, `.it`, and `.s3m`

By importing unsupported formats, you will not be able to utilize them, so make sure to convert those first.

You can find sound effects by navigating to **Chapter 8 | Sound Effects** inside the **Project** window to follow the book's material.

The import settings are used to control the compression of the audio data, which happens automatically on import. Compression allows you to reduce and control memory used by the audio data at a cost of dealing with performance overheads and reduction in sound quality. Unless you are looking for a way to optimize your level as much as possible, you can leave options at their default values.

The only option that can be of use at the introductory level is the **Force to Mono** checkbox that will downgrade mix channels to a single one.

At the bottom of **Import Settings**, you will find a **Preview** window with an audio wavelength, technical information, and play controls.

Play controls are listed in the following table:

Controls	Description
▶	This plays the sound track
⟳	This loops the track
◀)	This enables automatic play upon selecting **Audio Clip** in the **Hierarchy** window

One interesting trick that you can pull off with **Audio Clips** is to drag and drop them into the Scene. Dropping into the empty space you will create an empty GameObject with the **Audio Source** component and a dragged audio file as the **AudioClip** parameter assigned to it. Dropping on the existing GameObject will attach an **Audio Source** component to it and replace the top most **Audio Source** component that is already attached to it (if any).

2D versus 3D sounds

There are two kinds of sounds that are possible to emit by **Audio Sources** — those that play in the background with no indication of where they are coming from (ambient sounds and background music), and those that have a clear source with an ability to fade away with distance (conversation, alarm signal, speaker sound, and so on). In Unity, they are labeled as 2D and 3D sounds as a prime difference between them is a concept of depth.

You can make any kind of sound 2D or 3D by controlling the **Spatial Blend** parameter in the **Audio Source** component.

You can test the effect yourself by positioning **Audio Source** next to the listener in the scene and moving the slider left and right. 2D sound will have an effect as if it's coming from everywhere, while the location of 3D sound will be easy to point out.

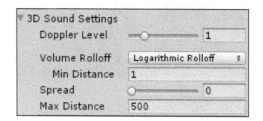

While the 2D sound can be easily controlled with the already discussed parameters, 3D sounds, due to their reliance on depth, have a set of their own parameters hidden under the **3D Sound Settings** drop-down list of the **Audio Source** component:

- **Doppler Level**: This controls the amount of influence that a relative velocity of listener or source has on the sound pitch. Think about the change in sound frequency a train has as it transitions from approaching to and passing right next to you. This parameter can influence that change.

- **Volume Rolloff**: These are presets for the change in the sound volume based on the distance between the source and a listener. You need to choose among **Logarithmic**, **Linear**, or **Custom** rolloffs:
  - **Linear**: This will make sound volume to tune down the further you are away from the source at a constant pace (linear reduction)

- ○ **Logarithmic**: This will increase the pace, the further you are from the source (the further you are, higher the pace of degradation)
  - ○ **Custom**: This will allow you to set your own preferences, which we will look into shortly
- **Min Distance**: This is a distance at which **Volume Rolloff** will start to take effect.
- **Spread**: This controls the spread angle of the speaker space — useful for 3D and multi-channel sounds.
- **Max Distance**: This is a distance at which you stop controlling the sound rolloff. It's not necessarily a distance at which the sound is not playing anymore.

The following is a demonstration of minimum and maximum distance:

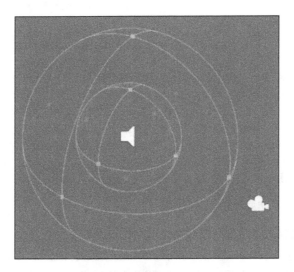

As you can see, there are two spheres around **Audio Source**. The inner sphere is a boundary of **Min Distance** (currently set to 1) and the outer sphere is a boundary for **Max Distance** (currently set to 2, but it's usually defaulted to 500, which means you won't normally see it). The **Main Camera** object with a listener is located outside of both spheres; however, if we have **Logarithmic Rolloff** selected, we will still be able to hear the sound playing. Should we switch to **Linear Rolloff**, the sound will disappear as soon as we get out of the **Max Distance** range.

The reason why this is happening is quite simple: the rolloff for the volume (and a few other parameters) is controlled by the graph at the bottom of the **Audio Source** component:

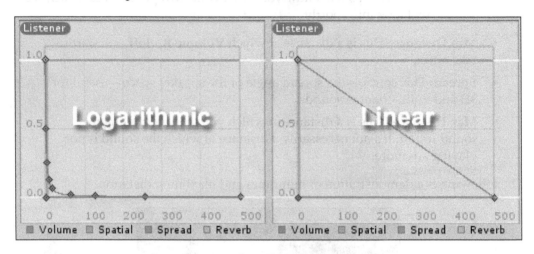

The graph is drawn as a relation between distance to the **Listener** (x axis) and a numeric value of the parameter (y axis), in this case, **Volume**. Choosing **Logarithmic** or **Linear** will give you one of the two available presets for **Volume Rolloff**. Attempting to manually modify curve values will cause it to automatically switch to **Custom Rolloff**. By the way, rolloff curve controls are identical to those of custom **Animation** curves discussed in *Chapter 4, Dealing with Basic Animations*, which means you can add, manipulate keys and control the curves with tangents to tailor it to your needs.

Introduction to audio mixer

Creating rich audio effects and making them work is a tough task. Earlier, control over complex sound systems at runtime required a lot of programming support; besides that, the pipeline itself felt disorganized as audio designers would have all those individual audio sources stationed around the level, turning the process of managing them into quite a headache. Thankfully, developers at **Unity Technologies** realized this issue and managed to come up with a solution in the form of the audio mixer.

How does it work?

Making its debut with the release of Unity 5, the audio mixer came a long way in addressing most of the annoying issues associated with audio management. We will see the application of that in a following example; however, first, let's take a look at what it consists of:

1. Open the window called **Audio Mixer** from the **Window** tab at the top menu.

2. Once you get there, click on the **+** sign next to **Mixers**.

This will create our first audio mixer that we will use to explain the general functionality of this feature. Just like any other window in Unity, you can dock it wherever you feel comfortable with, and you can also switch between two layouts: **Vertical** and **Horizontal** by right-clicking on the window and selecting the option from the drop-down menu.

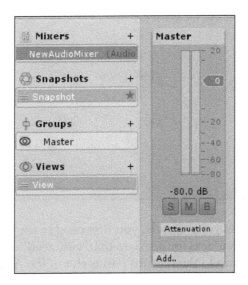

You should be able to see four elements that are the core of the audio mixing system as discussed in the following:

- **Mixers**: They are the assets that are holding all the elements of the **Audio Mixer** system. Upon creation, they appear in the **Project** window.

- **Snapshots**: They capture presets for all parameters in the **Audio Mixer**. They are very useful; however, they can only be swapped at runtime with code.

- **Groups**: They are the bread and butter of audio mixing. This is where the majority of all the parameters and controls are housed. They can store references to the **Audio Sources** or control other groups by assigning effects and building hierarchies with them.

- **Views**: They are filters that allow you to showcase any particular set of groups that you are currently interested in. To do that, simply create a new **View** and hide all groups that you aren't interested in by clicking on the eye icon next to them.

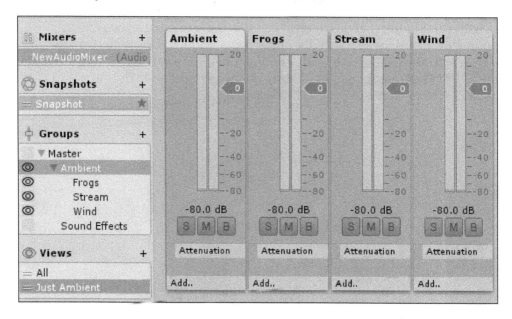

Before you are able to mix your sounds, you first need to set a reference for **Audio Sources** to a particular **Group**. To do that, you need to assign or drag and drop the **Audio Group** to the **Output** parameter of the **Audio Source** that you want to modify.

Naturally, you will need to create an **Audio Group** for it first, in the same way you created a **Mixer** (by hitting the plus sign).

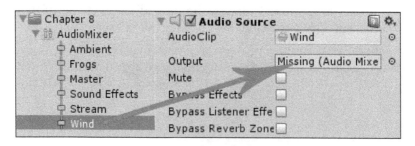

Now, everything you do with the group will directly affect the connected audio source.

Let's start practicing with the audio mixer from here by creating a mix of ambient sounds in our outdoor scene:

1. Find the audio files by navigating to **Chapter 8 | Sound Effects** and add the following into the scene by dragging and dropping them into an empty area: **Wind, Birds, River, Waterfall** and **Background Music**.

2. Create an audio group for each of them in the **Audio Mixer**.

3. Assign audio groups to their respective **Audio Sources**.

4. Check the **Loop** box in all the created **Audio Sources**.

5. Set **Spatial Blend** of **Waterfall** sound to full 3D and **River** sound in the middle.

You should have something similar to the following screenshot by the end of it:

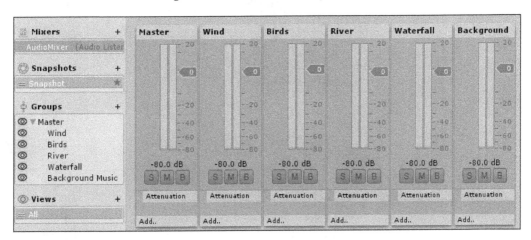

Make sure that all the created audio groups are children to the master group and not of each other. When adding a new audio group, you should have the master group selected, as the audio mixer will always add a new group as a child of the currently selected one.

Once you enter a **Play** mode, you will regret not turning your speakers down because these sounds will start playing simultaneously creating a terrible noise that is yet to be properly tuned.

Modifying at runtime

Imagine if all the changes done during the runtime are reverted as soon as you go out of the **Play** mode. It has its benefits when dealing with visual objects, but with sounds, all we can see are parameters, and we can only change them if we are aware of the final result or just trying to find the right values. For that purpose, in the **Play** mode, you are allowed to edit **Audio Mixers** at runtime and save changes after getting out of the **Play** mode, with the **Edit** in **Play** mode button. It will appear in the **Audio Mixer** window as soon as you enter the **Play** mode.

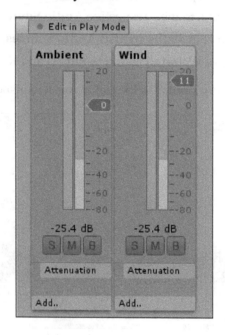

Now you can adjust all the sounds in the mix according to your preferences. There are three other options that you can use at this stage to help you find the right settings for each individual sound and they can be accessed via three buttons at the bottom of the **Audio Group**, which are listed in the following table:

Buttons	Description
S M B	**Solo** will mute all other groups and play sounds of this group.
S M B	**Mute** will mute the selected group.
S M B	**Bypass** will ignore the effects applied to this group

Once you are finished with editing, you can place 3D sounds like **River** and **Waterfall** in their respected places in the level.

Filters and reverb zones

One of the main tools of tuning sounds is to apply various effects through **Filters** and **Reverb Zones**.

Filters can be attached to the specific **Audio Sources** via components or **Sound Groups** inside **Audio Mixer** with an **Add...** button at the bottom of the group.

 Adding **Filters** to **Audio Groups** is the preferred way. Filters as components exist for backward compatibility with older versions of Unity that didn't have audio mixers

Filters affect specific audio sources that they are assigned to (and its hierarchy, in a case of audio groups). We will not discuss any filter in particular, due to their situational nature; however, keep in mind that the order in which you apply filters does matter a great deal, you might not always perceive the difference, but it is there.

Reverb zones are slightly different; they are the spherical volumes (components) that you place in the level to add a reverb to the **Audio Sources** if the **Audio Listener** is within the **Reverb Zone** area.

Let's take a look at the example in the **Cave** scene inside the **Chapter 8** folder. In the scene, we have a **Waterfall Audio Source**, a **Reverb Zone** inside of a cave and an **Audio Listener** attached to the character. The listener is clearly outside of the **Reverb Zone** area; therefore, the reverb will not be applied. However, as soon as a character moves in, the reverb will start being applied to the **Audio Sources** that it can hear. In other words, it doesn't change any **Audio Source** in particular, but applies a reverb to a **Listener** affecting how we can hear sounds.

The reason why I said, *it will start being applied* is because there are two parameters of the **Reverb Zone** component that control this transition: **Min Distance** and **Max Distance** between them, the reverb effect goes from 0 percent (beyond max distance) to 100 percent (within min distance).

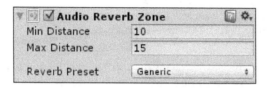

Reverb zones are used to add environmental effects to the sounds. The character enters a cave that has a reverb zone inside of it, with the appropriate settings that will add an acoustic effect to everything he hears.

 You can choose the available effects from the **Reverb Presets** drop-down menu, or design your own by choosing the **User** option and tweaking the sliders.

Enter the **Play** mode and navigate the character into the cave. Once the character is inside the **Reverb Zone**, add the **Lowpass Filter** to the master group via the **Add...** button at the bottom of it. You should immediately hear the difference and a greater feeling that you've entered the cave.

There are some scenarios where you don't want sounds to be affected by the reverb zone and filters, more specifically; the background music. To exclude specific audio sources from being affected by the reverb zones and filters, check both **Bypass Reverb Zones** and **Bypass Effects** boxes of the **Audio Source** component that plays background music in your level.

Summary

Unity's audio system has a low entry barrier. Beginner users will appreciate a user-friendly interface and simple pipelines, while advanced users will find a very flexible tool that can create impressive effects out of the box. The Introduction of the audio mixer gave a great amount of freedom to the **Audio Designers** with an added support for custom user plugins that will allow expanding the available capabilities even further.

That being said, some amount of coding is still required in order to make sound effects play at the right place and at the right time. Unfortunately, that is also the case with our next topic, in which we will discuss how to create and configure particle effects.

Exploring the Particle System

9

Particles are fun, they allow us to simulate various kinds of visual effects that greatly enhance the viewing experience, be it fire, fog, magic, or just a gigantic explosion.

In this chapter, you will learn about:

- Particles and what they are
- How to use a particle editor in Unity
- How to create your own custom particle for the level

The general rule of thumb when working with particles is figuring out what you want to create and then go, step by step, configuring a single parameter at a time. Try different things, experiment, and you will be surprised at the results you can achieve with a few textures and a well-tuned particle system alone.

What are particles?

Particles are sprites or game objects that are created and controlled by the particle system to simulate various graphical effects, mainly chaotic, natural phenomenon's, or chemical reactions that will otherwise be difficult to recreate with conventional rendering techniques. Fire, sparks of electricity, fireworks, dust, rain, snow, explosions, and magic spells—all can be created with the use of the particle system that is available in Unity.

I encourage you to take a look at some of the examples of particle systems available in Unity's standard package by navigating to **Assets | Import Package | Particle Systems**.

My personal favorite is the fireworks particle, it can be found under **Standard Assets | ParticleSystems | Prefabs | Fireworks**. In order to see a particle system in action, simply drag and drop it into the scene and keep it active (selected).

The best part is that all of that beauty can be created by an artist without a single line of code. How? Well, we have an amazing particle editor to thank.

The particle editor

Just like with most Unity functionalities, you can create a particle system as a standalone GameObject by navigating to **GameObject | Particle System** or attach it to an existing GameObject as a component by navigating to **AddComponent | Effects | Particle System**. It is quite a useful functionality for something like muzzle flashes from a gunfire. However, let's stick to the first option for now and take a look at how the particle system operates.

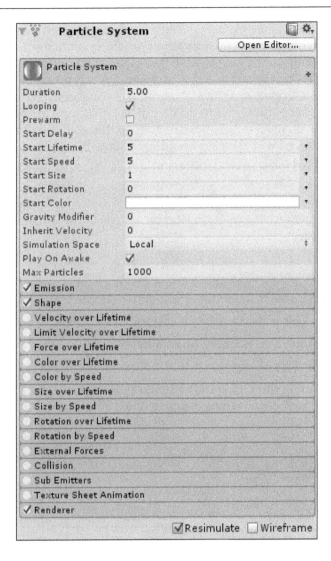

The particle system control is an unfolded section at the top. This is where most basic and important controls are located that every particle system must have, so it makes sense to pause here and take a brief look at them:

- **Duration**: This determines how long this system will be emitting particles. This helps to control the length of one-shot effects, such as explosions.

- **Looping**: As you might guess, this checkbox makes **Particle System** emit over and over again. Apart from direct application, it's also useful to keep checked when testing particles for a continuous effect.

- **Prewarm**: This allows you to start the particle system in the middle of a simulation. Whenever you activate a **Particle System**, it will start emitting the particles from the source, and, if, let's say, you've created an explosion and want the dust cloud to rise up immediately, **Prewarm** will allow you to achieve that. **Prewarm** allows you to skip gradual emitting and start off right when the first particle gets to the end of its lifetime cycle. In order to activate **Prewarm**, you need to have **Looping** on. In the case of explosions, the code usually takes care of toggling **Looping** to allow **Prewarm** to be useable.

- **Start Delay**: This is the opposite to **Prewarm**. This parameter allows you to set a timed delay to emission of particles upon activation, useful if you have multiple particle types emitting by the same system and you want to set an offset for them (first explosion later on—dust cloud). This is disabled if you have **Prewarm** checked.

- **Start Lifetime**: This determines how long each emitted particle will exist in the scene before disappearing.

- **Start Speed**: This is the initial speed of the particle upon emitting.

- **Start Size**: This is the initial scale factor of the particle.

- **Start Rotation**: This is the initial rotation.

- **Start Color**: This allows you to add a diffuse color to particles.

   One interesting thing to know about these **Start** parameters is that they can be defined as a variable number, generated from a range or a constant.

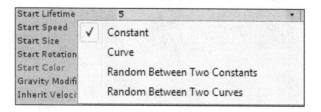

   By clicking on the triangle icon on the right side next to these parameters, you will open a drop-down menu with options to set these parameters:

- **Constant**: This is a default option where you set a constant number

- **Curve**: This option will allow you to graph a relation between this number and a Duration parameter

- **Random Between Two Constants** and **Random Between Two Curves**: These are the extensions of the previous two options that allow you to randomly pick a number from a certain range

A sound advice would be not to go too crazy with these numbers early on to avoid frustration given the number of options; it's easy to mess up.

- **Gravity Modifier**: This sets the influence of the gravity on particles.

- **Inherit Velocity**: This one is a little bit harder to explain, as it's only useful in very specific situations. Let's say we have a magical carriage on the move, perhaps it's taking Cinderella to the ball, and there are magical sparks emitting all around it and they form some kind of a trail as it moves. If we try to emit these particles right now, we will get a trail of them behind the carriage; however, if we tweak this parameter, the emitted particles will inherit part of the object's velocity and will start to get ahead of it. In order for it to work properly, you need to move the GameObject via a rigidbody and **Simulation Space** needs to be set to **World**. More about **rigidbody** component in the next chapter.

- **Simulation Space**: Will the particles be simulated in the **World** or **Local** space? A running and shooting soldier emitting muzzle fire effects should be simulated in Local space in order to move with the gun, but something like bullet shells should drop on the ground where they were emitted from, so they are better off being simulated in the world space.

- **Play On Awake**: This starts the particle automatically upon object instantiation or entering the **Play** mode.

- **Max Particles**: This is the maximum number of particles emitted from this source that can exist in the scene at any moment in time. Very useful for optimization—if the particle limit is met, the system will put emitting on a temporary halt.

The rest of the options under **Particle System Control** are optional modules that can be activated to add additional layers of control to the particle system. We will look into some of them in the next section of this chapter, but, ultimately, they are quite self-explanatory.

The latter part is a **Particle Editor** that can be entered by pressing a corresponding button, **Open Editor…**, in the top-right corner of the component. The **Particle Editor** gives you control over multiple particle systems that are connected by the hierarchy; it's just a more comfortable way of dealing with particle systems.

Creating a waterfall

In this section, we will challenge ourselves to create a particle system for our level, namely a waterfall, nothing crazy, but something that we will be able to create without any code support, relying only on texture work and a built-in particle system.

Setting up assets

Let's begin with setting up the assets that will be required for a creation of this particle effect and taking a closer look at them:

1. Create a **Particle System** in the scene by navigating to **GameObject | Particle System**.

2. Go to **Chapter 9 | Waterfall** to locate a material and a prefab by the name **Waterfall**.

3. Assign a created particle system to the **Waterfall** prefab.

That is literally everything we need to create in order to start working on the **Particle System**. This is how your **Waterfall** folder should look at this point:

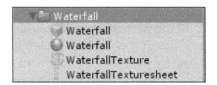

The **WaterfallTexture** image is going to be used for our first iteration of the waterfall. It's a very simple grayscale image 128 x 128 (using low resolution square textures for particles is highly recommended); in order to be properly utilized, we need to make sure that the alpha channel is generated from the grayscale by checking two checkboxes in the **WaterfallTexture Import Settings**: **Alpha from Grayscale** and **Alpha is Transparent**.

Needless to say, you can also use an image that contains an alpha without any need to generate it in Unity. This will also allow you to add a color to it that is different to white, but, in this case, we have an opportunity to compensate for that in a different manner.

Lastly, we need to configure the material:

1. Assign the **WaterfallTexture** to the **Albedo** parameter of the **Waterfall** material.

2. Set the **Rendering Mode** parameter to **Cutout**.

WaterfallTexturesheet will come into play later.

Configuring the particle system

Going back to our particle system, let's take a look at what modules and parameters we will need to configure in order to make it look like a waterfall. I will go through them in the same order I did for creation and talk through the process of utilizing different modules in order to create a proper effect.

Emitting direction

We will make sure that our particles are emitting in the correct direction. First of all, I don't like the fact that my particles are flying up in the air as they are emitting. If nature taught me anything, it's that water falls down. We will fix this nuisance by setting **Gravity Modifier** to 1.85 (hereinafter, numbers we generated after spending some time tweaking and trying to come up with the best result and are not staple).

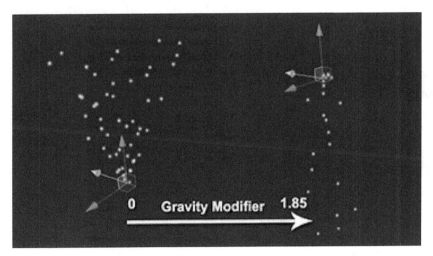

Now, the emitting source. By default, the particle system is emitting particles in a cone-shaped direction. This is not something that we want for our waterfall, so we should go into the **Shape** module and change the **Shape** parameter to **Box**. The Box's shape can be altered via transform and the parameters inside the **Shape** module. Personally, I've set the **Box Y** parameter to 10 and **Rotation** in the **Transform** component to (45, 0, 90).

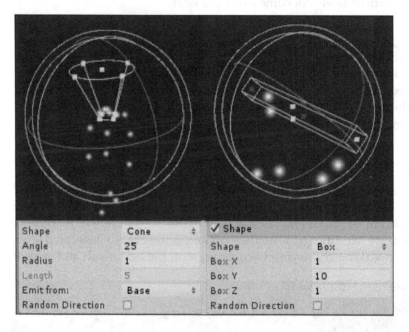

Shape	Cone		✓ Shape		
Angle	25		Shape	Box	
Radius	1		Box X	1	
Length	5		Box Y	10	
Emit from:	Base		Box Z	1	
Random Direction	☐		Random Direction	☐	

Some of you might wonder at this point why we added a **Gravity Modifier** if we could simply rotate the box to change the emitting direction. That is true; however, choosing this way allows us to get this nice arc, as particles are emitted on a certain angle and are forced down by gravity.

Configuring particles

It is about time to assign the material to particles and to see how that's going to work for us.

In order to do that, we will go into a **Renderer** module and assign the **Waterfall** material to the **Material** parameter.

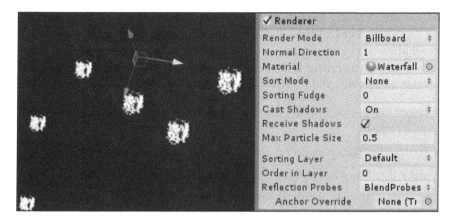

It looks terrible, nothing like the waterfall at all. However, we are getting there; let's address the issues one by one. The first obvious observation is that they are way too small. Therefore, we shall increase their initial size by changing the **Start Size** parameter to 5 (up from 1). This is a little better, but they aren't occupying enough space as of yet, and we can still see the gaps at the source. To address this issue, we will simply emit more of them, by going to the **Emission** module and changing the **Rate** parameter to 20 (up from 10).

In this case, we have a large amount of water pouring into a thin air from some sort of a bucket and one interesting thing that water does in real-life situations is it proportionally fills up the entire space from the source to the impact zone (as long as water keeps coming). We can't do quite the same thing in our case, because as you might imagine, stretching textures to variable sizes will produce unpredictable and, more often than not, horrible results. What we are going to do instead is partially stretch the texture until it starts to look similar to a real-life situation.

With that in mind, we are going to do the following:

1. Change the **Render Mode** parameter in the **Renderer** module to **Stretched Billboard**.

2. Change the **Length Scale** parameter to 1.5 (down from 2).

However, we aren't going to stop there, and we will go a little bit further by activating the **Size over Lifetime** module and tweaking some values there. This module will allow us to configure the scale of the particle throughout its lifecycle. We will use a curve to control it. In order to see the curve in the preview window, just click on it and perform the following steps:

1. Choose the second preset for the curve from right at the bottom of the curve editor.

2. Change the **Size** parameter at the top-left corner to 4 (up from 1)

3. Add a third key to the curve by right-clicking and choosing **Add Key**

4. Set keys to the following coordinates, from left to right (*x*,*y*):

   ○ (0.0,0.5)

   ○ (0.2,1.6)

   ○ (1.0,4.0)

Your curve should look similar to the following screenshot:

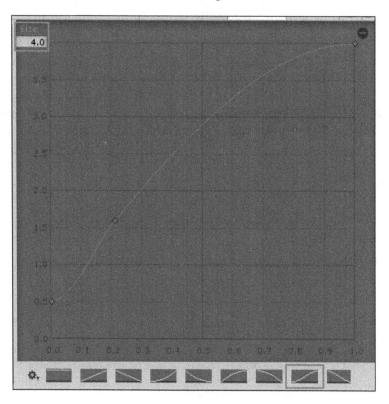

There we go! It looks much better now.

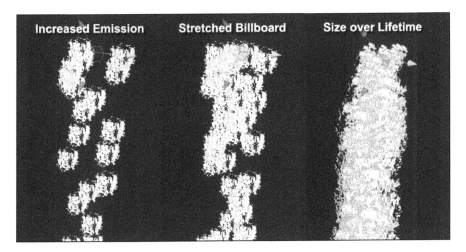

We are almost there; a few more touches are left.

Polishing

Right now, the waterfall is way too predictable; it's kind of boring to see the same texture emitted over and over again. To add some variety, we are going to introduce a texture sheet with multiple texture variation. To start off, let's do the following:

1. Assign the **WaterfallTexturesheet** to the **Albedo** parameter of the **Waterfall** material.
2. While we're on that, let's also change the color of **Albedo** to something bluish.
3. Activate the **Texture Sheet Animation** module inside **Particle System**.
4. Change the **Tiles Y** parameter to 5 (up from 1).
5. Set the **Animation** parameter to **Single Row**.

Now, we finally have our **Waterfall**:

In order to control its length, we can simply change the **Start Lifetime** parameter.

However, let's step back a little bit and take a look at how the texture sheet animation worked its miracles for us, and how we can utilize it in different situations.

Texture sheet animation

The texture sheet works very similar to the flares textures, and any other animation texture sheet. Inside the module, we are specifying the number of square tiles that our sheet consists of (X and Y of **Tiles** parameter).

The **Animation** parameter allows us two options to choose from: we are either using images from the **Whole Sheet** or utilizing a **Single Row** of images. The latter enables the **Random Row** parameter that allows us to randomly choose a row for the texture. In our case, it works quite well since we have five waterfall images lined up in a single column representing rows of their own. The size of the texture in question is 128 x 512, and that's why for the **Tiles** parameter we've assigned values of 5 to Y and 1 to X. Unity will then come up with a conclusion that the default size of a single image is 128 x 128 pixels and that there are five of them along the y axis.

In the case of a **Waterfall**, we aren't actually animating anything, but simply taking random images from **Texture Sheet** to create variety. However, if you have a ready texture sheet, you can control animation with the **Frame over Time** parameter via curves or constants.

The last parameter, **Cycles**, specifies how many times the animation will play over the lifetime of the particle, combined with the **Start Lifetime** and **Frame over Time** parameters; it will allow you to control the animation speed.

Coin particles

As for the practical example, I would like you to create a particle system that will rain money upon opening the chest, like the one in the following screenshot:

Everything required to create this particle effect can be found by navigating to **Chapter 9 | CoinParticle**.

So, the idea is that as soon as we enter the **Play** mode and press the space bar, the chest will play opening animation, and, at that moment, the particle system should start emitting coins in the air that will eventually fall down, forced by the gravity, and roll onto the floor.

Here is a list of particle system modules that you will require to create that particle effect:

1. **Emission**: This module is a kind of obvious choice—those coins need to be emitted after all.

2. **Shape**: This module is the same as the previous one, which requires source and direction to be properly configured.

3. **Rotation by Speed**: This module is the one we didn't talk about, but it is quite simple to use. It changes the angular velocity of a particle based on the **Speed Range** parameters inside the module.

4. **Collision**: This module will allow you to achieve the rolling effect. By changing collision to **World**, the coins will collide with the ground. The way they respond to the collision is controlled by the **Dampen** and **Bounce** parameters.

5. **Renderer**: The only thing you will need to modify in this module and is the material used to emit coins.

These five modules should be enough. Once you are finished, all that is left to do is as follows:

1. Find the script called **OpenChest.cs** and assign it as a component to the Chest GameObject in the Scene (by dragging and dropping or by navigating to **Add Component | Scripts | Open Chest**).

2. This script has one parameter called **Coin Particle**, drag and drop your particle system to it.

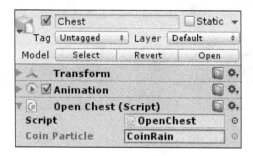

Now you can test your particle system by entering the **Play** mode and pressing the space bar.

Summary

The Unity particle system is a very powerful tool for creating various types of particle effects that can produce impressive results out of the box without coding. It might seem a little confusing at first, but once you figure out what you need, it's easy to find which parameters to modify in order to achieve whatever effect you have in mind. The important part to remember is to modify one parameter at a time to avoid confusion.

Unity standard assets contain a good starting set of frequently used particle systems that you can use in your level or reverse engineer to figure out a way to create your own.

In the last chapter, we will look at more ways to enhance our level before publishing.

10
Final Editing and Build

Level creation is coming to the finish line, and it's time to talk about some of the things that are available in Unity to tailor a better user experience.

In this chapter, you will learn about:

- Rigidbodies
- Available quality setting
- Setting up key bindings
- Scene configuration
- Level loading and streaming
- Level publishing

Most of the functionalities that will we look into in this chapter is what makes Unity so powerful and popular in the independent development scene. These out of the box solutions to mundane functionalities are very useful and will allow you to save a lot of time mid development, however, they are not perfect panacea. Those looking for powerful presentation and maximum optimization will have to do extra polishing.

Rigidbodies

It is about time we finalize our character and make him move around, taking landscape into consideration. For that, we need to rely on physics and, more specifically, a component that will enable our GameObject to follow physical laws — rigidbody.

Right now, the character that we've imported and set up animations for in *Chapter 5, Invite Your Characters to Unity* and *Chapter 6, Using Mecanim for Advanced Animations* is completely ignoring the environmental obstacles around itself and walks through walls like a ghost. To demonstrate how rigidbodies work, we will eliminate this issue by allowing our character to behave naturally and react to the environment properly. We will do this in four steps, and I would strongly recommend you to test the character in **Play** mode after each step to see the difference for yourself:

1. Attach the **Rigidbody** component to the **Robot** GameObject in the **Scene** window (**Add Component | Physics | Rigidbody**). This will allow gravity to influence our character model.

2. Check the **Bake into pose** parameters under **Root Transform Position (Y)** for all animation clips used for character animations. This will make sure that animations aren't controlling the *Y* transform for the character and allow it to go up and down via physics.

3. Add the **Capsule** collider to the **Robot** GameObject. This will prevent our character from falling under the ground. Make sure to configure it properly to match the robot's silhouette as close as possible, this will be important when it will start to calculate the collision.

4. Check all three boxes of the **Freeze Rotation** parameter (*X*, *Y*, *Z*). Doing this will prevent the character from falling down when moving. All robot rotations at this point will be controlled by the animations and scripts.

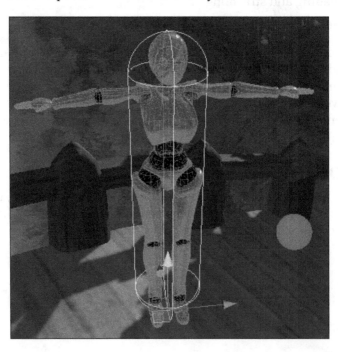

Testing the robot in **Play** mode should have revealed that, upon adding the **Rigidbody** component, the behavior of our character didn't change. Normally, that is not the case. Any object that has rigidbody added to it starts to get affected by gravity and falls to the ground. However, since our character is playing animations, they overwrite the gravity effect, thus keeping the robot floating.

When animations are baked into the pose, they are not affecting the objects transform and, therefore, allow gravity to have its way with a robot, causing it to fall.

Being affected by physics is good, but falling through the ground isn't. Why is this happening, and why isn't rigidbody doing anything to prevent it? The issue here is that rigidbody doesn't know that the robot is colliding with another object. In *Chapter 2, Importing and Configuring Props*, we talked about colliders and that they exist mainly to register when colliders intersect each other. Rigidbody reads this information and communicates to the GameObject how to react when an intersection occurs; in this case, it causes them to collide.

The parameters of rigidbody are explained in the following:

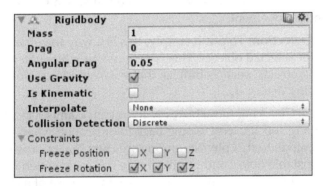

- **Mass**: This determines the mass of an object to help evaluate its physical attributes.
- **Drag and Angular Drag**: This drags coefficients of a rigidbody. 0 causes it to have no damping.
- **Use Gravity**: This causes the GameObject to be affected by gravity. Gravity force can be configured by going to **Edit | Project Settings | Physics**.
- **Is Kinematic**: Checking this box will stop GameObject from being driven by the physics engine. It might sound like it defeats the purpose of having rigidbody attached in the first place. In reality it does not; there are at least three reasons to do so:
  - Enable collision when we are moving a GameObject with transform (via code).

○ Rigidbody component is rather expensive; making it kinematic will make it significantly cheaper.

○ Rigidbodies are detectable by triggers. This requires some explanation.

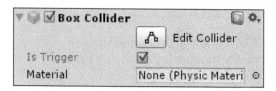

Triggers are colliders with the enabled **Is Trigger** parameter, which turns them into areas that can detect when GameObjects enter it, and stay there, or leave it. Triggers are invaluable for level design as they are literally used to trigger most of the code in the level. There is one condition, though, in order to be detectable by the trigger area, the GameObject must have a rigidbody attached to it.

- **Interpolate**: This is used to smooth out the transform in case there is jerkiness in rigidbody movement.

- **Collision Detection**: To put it simply, this is a way to enhance collision detection for selected objects. This is very useful when you are dealing with fast moving objects, such as bullets, that we need to occasionally go through without being detected.

- **Constraints**: Checking these boxes will prevent GameObject translation or rotation along specific axes. Going back to our robot: when we've attached a capsule collide to it, a physics engine sees just that, a capsule. A capsule is a very unstable object and might simply roll away when it collides with something. This is not what we wish to see in the case of a robot, which is exactly why we put constrain on those axes – to prevent that from happening to our robot and keep it standing straight at all times.

That will finalize our character; it's now capable to follow the landscape properly and even step over small obstacles.

Project settings

Before publishing our level, we need to spend some time configuring settings according to our needs. In this section, we will look into the settings available under **Edit | Project Settings** of the top menu, namely, **Input** and **Quality**.

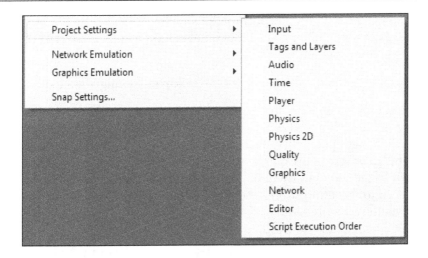

We'll go to **Input** first. Just like it sounds, input contains the entire array of key bindings available in the level.

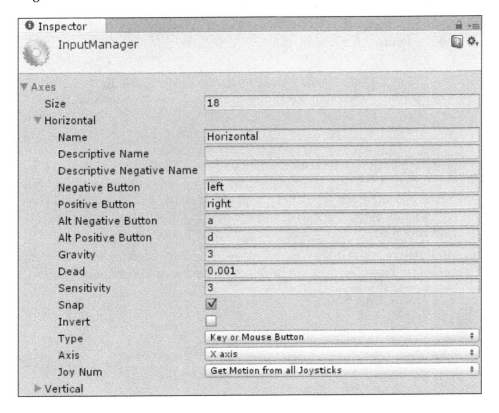

Just like as any array in Unity, the number of slots is controlled by the **Size** parameter. By default, Unity has 18 binded keys that you can use out of the box or change based on your needs.

In order to properly set up keys, we have the following configurations:

- **Name**: Obviously, this determines how the button will be named. However, there are few things to consider when deciding the name for the button. First of all, changing the name of the button mid-development can cause some scripts to break, as programmers will most likely reference **Name** of the input in the code (and will be correct to do so as it allows for simple button reconfiguration for players), so make sure to agree on the proper naming conventions beforehand.

- **Descriptive Name** and **Descriptive Negative Name**: This mentions the names of the input that will be displayed to the player in the **Input** window of **Unity Player**. Changing **Descriptive Name** will not cause the code to break and you can configure it at any time.

- **Positive button**: This determines which button is assigned to this input. A slight inconvenience is that you have to manually type in the name of the key in order for it to work.

> To find out the proper naming for the keys, refer to the Unity documentation at http://docs.unity3d.com/Documentation/ Manual/Input.html. For the controller, simply Google the controller layout for Unity.

- **Negative Button**: This is used when you have another action that is opposite to this one. A primary example will be movement controls: walking right can be considered as a positive input and walking left as negative. Player will see this as two options in the key binding menu, **Horizontal (+)** and **Horizontal (-)**.

- **Alt Positive** and **Alt Negative Buttons**: These are used for secondary input variation. This way, you can have keys from the keyboard and joystick assigned to this input.

- **Sensitivity and Gravity**: This determines the sensitivity of the input. The former determines how fast in Unity seconds the value of the input will go to max upon triggering it, and the latter determines how fast it will return to 0. For something like movement, you want this to be fairly low, and high for something like shooting.

- **Dead**: This is the size of the analog deadzone and is used for joysticks and other devices with analog input.

- **Snap**: This is a very useful checkbox for smoothing in transition if you have positive and negative input configured. What it does is snap input value to 0 whenever the opposite button is used and continue from there without **Gravity** having the effect.

- **Invert**: This changes positive input to negative.

- **Type**: This determines the type of input that is registered. **Key and Mouse Button** is used for button pressing, **Mouse Movement** for mouse position change, and **Scrollwheel or Joystick Axis** for joystick.

- **Axis**: This determines the axis used by a joystick or scroll wheel (if you are using **Mouse Movement Type**). If **Axis** is selected, you don't need to specify **Positive** or **Negative** buttons as input will be read from the joystick axis.

- **Joy Num**: This helps you to specify which joystick to reference for this input. Needless to say, it is a situational option.

By default, players can choose between different quality settings when launching the game in Unity by selecting one of the options from the drop-down menu. These options can be listed and modified if you go to **Edit | Project Settings | Quality**.

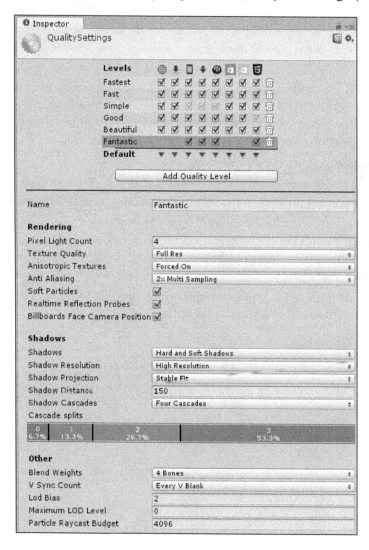

In the **Quality** window, you can create a custom list of settings for your game and can customize the settings for **Rendering, Shadows,** and **Other** options that will be associated with it (presets essentially).

Scene configuration

Having one beautiful level is wonderful, but what if we have more - how do we connect them to ensure that the player sees them all? The process is actually quite simple and doesn't require much work from our side: any kind of level loading is done via code anyway. However, there are still things that we are required to take care of regardless.

As you must have noticed already, the levels are represented by scenes in Unity, and during development, we could have a large number of scenes piled up, some of which we would like to see in the final game, while others exist for testing purposes or prototypes. In order to avoid unnecessary assets being added to our final build, we need to list the scenes that will be included.

To do that, we go to **File | Build Settings...** of the top menu.

Right now, we are only interested at the top part of this window, but we shall revisit it later and talk about the rest of the options in the future. **Scenes In Build** is a list of all scenes that will be added to our current build of the game and allows us to manage them for different releases. There are few actions that we can do from here:

- To add a scene to the list, simply open the scene in Unity and hit the **Add Current** button in the **Build Settings** window
- To remove the scene from the build, uncheck the box to the left of the scene
- To remove the scene from the list, select the scene and hit the *Delete* key.

Should that be it, the **Scenes In Build** window will be quite useless. Its major purpose is to assign the scenes an integer number that will be used to reference it in the code. Every consecutive scene will have an incrementally bigger number. In order to change the number, we need to change the ordering of the scene by holding and dragging them up or down through the list. It is a simple, but quite effective, method.

To proceed with the example of moving from level to level, do the following:

1. Go into your created level and add it to the list.

2. Open the **Chapter_10_Scene** folder inside the **Chapter10** folder and add it to the list as well.

3. Return to your level, drag and drop a **Level_Exit** prefab into the scene (can be found inside the **Chapter10** folder).

4. Position it in a way so that your character is able to reach it by walking.

Make sure that both level checkboxes are checked and that they are assigned correct numbers inside the **Scenes In Build** window, as displayed on the following screenshot:

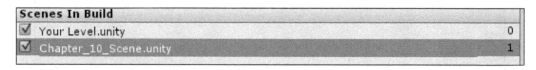

Now that everything is set up, we will be able to test level loading.

Level loading and streaming

In Unity, levels can be loaded in four different ways:

- Loading: This destroys all the objects in the current scene and loads the new one with the loading screen. Optionally, you can specify which objects you don't want to be destroyed from the previous level by code.

- Loading additively: Unlike normal loading, this doesn't destroy the objects present in the previous level, but adds new objects to them.

- Loading asynchronously: This loads levels in the background, allowing you to play the game simultaneously or use a loading screen.

- Loading additively asynchronously: This works in the same way as asynchronous loading, but it preserves the objects from the previous level.

The differences are minor, but they can change the way you build your levels based on the type of the gameplay you are aiming to create.

To test out how level loading works, navigate your character to the **Level_Exit** prefab that you placed earlier, and a normal loading should initiate.

Level loading limitations

The greatest limitation to level loading comes from real-time global illumination. If you remember, when we looked at how it works in *Chapter 7, Lighting up the World,* we discovered that Realtime GI requires precomputing to work properly at runtime, which cannot be achieved if you are aiming for the procedurally generated level.

A similar issue will be encountered should you choose to add more items to the already existing level. The solution to that would be to bake the lightmap and then deactivate the items you wish to add.

Lastly, there is a modular level generation when you have a set of environments that you are planning to reuse many times to create something like an endless runner type of game. The challenge here is hiding the seams between different modules.

Publishing the level

Finally, we get to the last point — publishing and releasing our level as a standalone application, which takes us back to the **Build Settings** window.

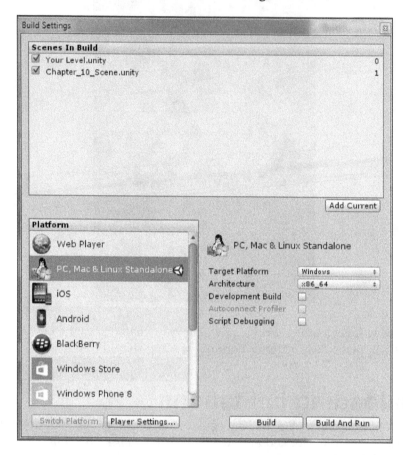

When you first launch the window, your default platform will be set to the **PC, Mac & Linux Standalone** option. In order to change the platform, you can change it either with the **Target Platform** drop-down menu on the right (options between Windows, Mac, and Linux) or select the desired platform from the list on the right and click on the **Switch Platform** button. Having the desired platform set for your level will allow Unity to issue warnings whenever you are trying to utilize something that is not supported by the selected platform.

Clicking on the **Player Settings...** button will open a set of settings that will help you to configure your game, such as adding information about the developer, the custom icons, the splash screen, the cursor, as well as the settings specific to every platform.

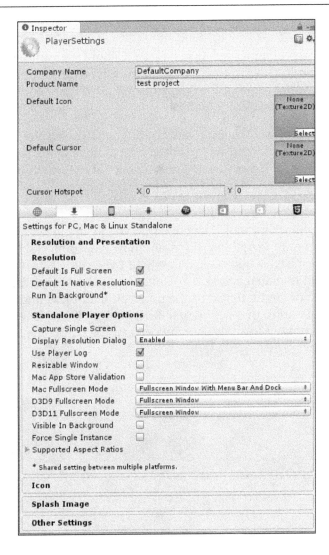

We won't change any of it, though, and will go with default settings. All that is left
is to:

1. Hit the **Build and Run** button.

2. Select the building directory.

3. Name the executable file.

4. Brag about your awesome level to friends (just don't forget to bring along the
   data folder with the executable file or it will not work).

That's it! Your level is now officially ready.

Summary

This concludes the development of our level. Publishing for multiple platforms with Unity is as simple as it can possibly be. Currently, Unity supports 21 platforms, some of them are available out of the box, while others require additional modules and third-party SDKs (consoles) to publish.

Out-of-the-box solutions for the input key binding, quality settings, and publishing are very useful, but generic, and will result in a lot of developers reinventing them to better suit their needs. However, that only applies at the end of development; mid-development you are still benefiting from them, especially if the level is developed for multiple platforms.

Thank you for finishing this book! We hope that you've managed to follow the book's tutorials, have tried out the optional tasks, and now feel comfortable inside of Unity. What you've learned in this book is just the tip of the iceberg when we compare it to everything that is available inside of Unity, and, who knows, Unity technologies improve their creation regularly, so by the time you read these lines, they might release yet another feature that will help to further simplify your working pipeline. However, until then, keep learning, keep experimenting, and have a great time working with Unity.

Index

Symbols

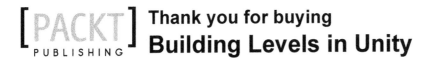

Thank you for buying
Building Levels in Unity

About Packt Publishing

Packt, pronounced 'packed', published its first book, *Mastering phpMyAdmin for Effective MySQL Management*, in April 2004, and subsequently continued to specialize in publishing highly focused books on specific technologies and solutions.

Our books and publications share the experiences of your fellow IT professionals in adapting and customizing today's systems, applications, and frameworks. Our solution-based books give you the knowledge and power to customize the software and technologies you're using to get the job done. Packt books are more specific and less general than the IT books you have seen in the past. Our unique business model allows us to bring you more focused information, giving you more of what you need to know, and less of what you don't.

Packt is a modern yet unique publishing company that focuses on producing quality, cutting-edge books for communities of developers, administrators, and newbies alike. For more information, please visit our website at www.packtpub.com.

Writing for Packt

We welcome all inquiries from people who are interested in authoring. Book proposals should be sent to author@packtpub.com. If your book idea is still at an early stage and you would like to discuss it first before writing a formal book proposal, then please contact us; one of our commissioning editors will get in touch with you.

We're not just looking for published authors; if you have strong technical skills but no writing experience, our experienced editors can help you develop a writing career, or simply get some additional reward for your expertise.

Getting Started with Unity

ISBN: 978-1-84969-584-8   Paperback: 170 pages

Learn how to use Unity by creating your very own "Outbreak" survival game while developing your essential skills

1. Use basic AI techniques to bring your game to life.

2. Learn how to use Mecanim; create states and manage them through scripting.

3. Use scripting to manage the graphical interface, collisions, animations, persistent data, or transitions between scenes.

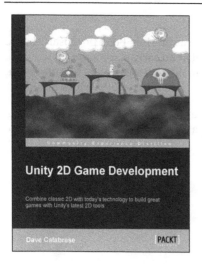

Unity 2D Game Development

ISBN: 978-1-84969-256-4   Paperback: 126 pages

Combine classic 2D with today's technology to build great games with Unity's latest 2D tools

1. Build a 2D game using the native 2D development support in Unity 4.3.

2. Create a platformer with jumping, falling, enemies, and a final boss.

3. Full of exciting challenges which will help you polish your game development skills.

Please check **www.PacktPub.com** for information on our titles

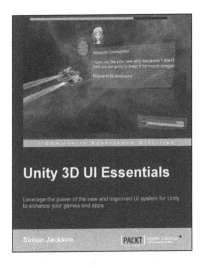

Unity 3D UI Essentials

ISBN: 978-1-78355-361-7   Paperback: 280 pages

Leverage the power of the new and improved UI system for Unity to enhance your games and apps

1. Discover how to build efficient UI layouts coping with multiple resolutions and screen sizes.

2. In-depth overview of all the new UI features that give you creative freedom to drive your game development to new heights.

3. Walk through many different examples of UI layout from simple 2D overlays to in-game 3D implementations.

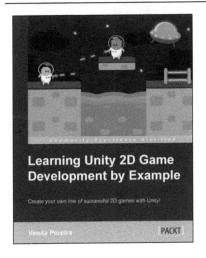

Learning Unity 2D Game Development by Example

ISBN: 978-1-78355-904-6   Paperback: 266 pages

Create your own line of successful 2D games with Unity!

1. Dive into 2D game development with no previous experience.

2. Learn how to use the new Unity 2D toolset.

3. Create and deploy your very own 2D game with confidence.

Please check **www.PacktPub.com** for information on our titles

www.ingramcontent.com/pod-product-compliance
Lightning Source LLC
Chambersburg PA
CBHW060530060326
40690CB00017B/3437